CONCERNING
SCANDALS

CONCERNING SCANDALS

by
John Calvin

Translated by
John W. Fraser

WILLIAM B. EERDMANS PUBLISHING COMPANY
GRAND RAPIDS, MICHIGAN

Library of Congress Cataloging in Publication Data

Calvin, John, 1509-1564.
  Concerning scandals.

  Translation of De scandalis.
  1. Reformed Church — Doctrinal and controversial works.
  2. Christian life — Reformed authors.
I. Title.
BX9420.D4213 248'.48'42 78-8675
ISBN 0-8028-3511-2

CONTENTS

TRANSLATOR'S PREFACE

1. Texts

This translation is based on the text in *Johannis Calvini, Opera Selecta*, edited by P. Barth and W. Niesel; Volume II, edited by P. Barth and Dora Scheuner (Munich, first edition, 1952; second edition, 1970, with correction list), pages 159-240. Their text is the Latin edition printed at Geneva by Jean Crespin (*Crispinus*) in 1550. There is also an edition of 1551 from the same printer. "The text of the 1551 edition agrees with that of 1550. In the notes we refer to some errors of the 1550 edition which were partly corrected at that time."[1] I have also noted these corrections.

Other Latin texts are to be found in collections of Calvin's works, including the Amsterdam edition, 1667, and the *Corpus Reformatorum*, Volume XXXVI, *Johannis Calvini, Opera quae supersunt omnia*, Volume VIII (Brunswick, 1870).

There are French versions of 1550 and 1551, also printed at Geneva by Crespin, and a version of 1560 printed at Geneva by Pinereul (*Pinerelus*). Occasional references to the French version by Barth-Scheuner have been incorporated in this translation. They do not, however, make note of unimportant verbal discrepancies.

Barth-Scheuner lists the libraries where extant copies of these earliest Latin and French editions are to be found.

---

1. *B-N*, p. 160.

2. Scripture

As in the recent translations of Calvin's New Testament Commentaries, the English Revised Version of the Bible has been used as a guide, and quoted when it agrees with Calvin's text. However, he often quotes in a rather free way, as if from memory, and in most instances his Latin has been translated directly. Barth-Niesel's citations of Calvin's Scripture references appear in parentheses within the text; my own Scripture citations, and my corrections of Barth-Niesel's, appear in square brackets.

3. General

For details of works by the Fathers, Reformation and other contemporaneous writers, the Barth-Scheuner volume should be consulted from the indications given in footnotes here. Sometimes it has been felt necessary to add some details about names of individuals or groups mentioned by Calvin, but this has not been done for well-known figures such as Luther, Sadoleto, Rabelais, or even Cochlaeus and Pighi, about whom information can easily be found.

Calvin's paragraphs are very long, often running to several pages. The majority have been broken up at what seem to be suitable places, and cross-headings have been inserted at the beginning of each of the original paragraphs to aid the cohesiveness of the argument.

To obtain the full value of Calvin's clear thought, it is best to stay as close as possible to what he says and not to attempt to paraphrase his Latin in any way. There are occasional ambiguities of expression in the Latin. But I have endeavored to make the translation readable in modern English.

Page references to the Barth-Scheuner text are given in the margin. Some misprints are noted in footnotes.

I am indebted to the Rev. Dr. T. H. L. Parker, University of Durham, for confirming the reference to a vestment on p. 112, and for providing the reference there and to P. Bunel on p. 24.

Manse of Farnell,   JOHN W. FRASER
BRECHIN, Angus.

ABBREVIATIONS

B-N	Barth-Niesel, Volume II.
Beveridge	*Institutes of the Christian Religion,* translated by H. Beveridge (Original 1845; London, 1953).
CR	*Corpus Reformatorum, Opera Calvini.*
E.Brit. Mic.	*Encyclopaedia Britannica* (15th ed., Chicago, 1974), *Micropaedia.*
Herminjard	A.-L. Herminjard, *Correspondance des réformateurs dans les pays de langue française* (Geneva, 1866-1897).
Inst.	John Calvin, *Institutes of the Christian Religion.*
NCMH	*New Cambridge Modern History* (Cambridge, 1957-58).
ODCC	*Oxford Dictionary of the Christian Church,* ed. F. L. Cross (2nd ed. Oxford, 1974).
RV	English *Revised Version.*
RSV	English *Revised Standard Version.*
Vulg. (WW)	Latin Vulgate (NT revision by John Wordsworth and Henry J. White, Oxford, 1911/1955).

INTRODUCTORY NOTE
by
P. BARTH and DORA SCHEUNER

FOR SEVERAL YEARS Calvin felt constrained to write a tract about
the vexations and stumbling blocks which certain men of the
Reformed Church, particularly the Franco-Gauls (*Francogalli*)
were obliged to endure because of their faith. When those
things were referred to the Reformer or reported to him by men
fleeing to Geneva, they moved him deeply and prompted him
not only to give them specific instruction but also to help and
encourage them.

In a letter to Farel dated September 1546,[1] he says that the
little book had then been begun, and several weeks later[2] that it
had to be laid aside because of his Commentary on the Epistle
to the Galatians. From a letter of August 1550,[3] we learn that it
was going to be completed in a short time.

This little work was dedicated to a very close friend of
Calvin, Laurent de Normandie, prefect of Noyon, Calvin's
birthplace, where Laurent was an attorney. Calvin declared
that, having been tried and tormented on account of his faith,
this man had such a nature that, guided by wisdom and
evangelical discernment, he withstood those stumbling blocks.
Laurent was also one of those exiles who finally received shelter
and a home in Geneva. Already in 1549, Calvin had dedicated
to him his "Advertissement contre l'astrologie iudicaire."[4,5]

1. *CR*, XII, p. 380, no. 826.
2. Calvin to Farel, 2 October, 1546, *CR*, XII, p. 390, no. 832.
3. Calvin to Farel, 19 August, 1550, *CR*, XIII, p. 623, no. 1398.
4. *CR*, VII, pp. xxxvii ff.
5. Calvin had also entrusted Laurent with the administration and discharge
of his will.

GREETINGS from JOHN CALVIN
TO THAT ESTIMABLE MAN OF MANY GIFTS
LAURENT DE NORMANDIE[1]

WHEN, FOR MANY REASONS, I made up my mind to dedicate some part of my labors to you, I considered that this little work should be chosen in preference to the rest, because your example can serve in no small degree as verification of the very teaching which it contains, and so create confidence in it. You have left your native land and come here to us as a voluntary exile. Because of that fact both of us are certainly very good witnesses of how much, and the way in which, Satan has violently attacked you with his stratagems; but there are also other people who are not ignorant of these things.

News of the death of your father came four months after you left home. It must have occurred to you, seeing that malicious tongues were at work, that the cause of his death could be put down to grief, so that the odium would fall wholly on your shoulders. A little later came the bitterest blow, when your wife, one that the best of men might wish for, was taken away in the very prime of life. Here again it was only to be expected that many different trials would arise to take the heart out of a man who was anything but insensitive. The calumnies of the wicked were now ringing in your ears to the effect that she had been dragged away from her native land, when the omens were unfavorable, to die, sick at heart, in an almost alien world. But what worried you more was the fact that it would have been

---

1. See also Calvin to Madame de Cany, 8 January, 1549, *CR,* XIII, pp. 144-147.

1

quite plausible if they were to make out that, by this sad event, the Lord had brought a curse on your plans. I make no mention of the innumerable stabs which it was only right for you to feel within yourself. For since a severe bereavement is a painful experience, the fact that you are deprived of life with a companion like her has meant more than shedding tears in your case. Finally, the funeral added greatly to the distress of your little daughter. At the same time Satan launched whatever attacks he could from different directions, so as to put an end to you by pressing hard upon a spirit that was already wounded. In a word, you have endured more troubles in six months than several people, of whose stout-heartedness much has been made, have had to put up with all their lives. But the most powerful scandal of all was the one that Satan craftily put in your way right at the start, for it might have forced you to retrace your steps. But, relying on the unconquerable power of the Spirit of God, you proved to everybody else that there is no obstacle so troublesome and difficult that it may not be surmounted with that same help.

At the same time you have gained experience of the kind of weapons with which the Lord usually equips his people for resistance, whenever he summons them to battle. I was the first person to break the news to you that your father was dead. And I then referred to the example of Abraham, whom his contemporaries could have called *his* father's murderer, because, as a result of Abraham's leaving home, Terah had died, when his son was still on the road. I remember your immediately making the point that, since you had God as a witness to what you had done and his approval of it, the calumnies of the wicked meant nothing to you. Only to grieve over the fact that you did not have the benefit of your father's companionship when you set out would have made your situation like Abraham's. I am certainly not accusing you of being so high and mighty as either to refuse to be associated with Abraham or to seek to avoid that ignominy which God honors with the highest praise. But your wife herself, before she left us, marvellously lightened and eased the grief of her departing. For no better antidote could have been wished for than those heroic words she uttered with her final breath, when, seizing my own hand, she gave thanks

163

2

to God, by whose hand she had been brought to that place where she could die in peace of mind; when, bewailing in her heart the circumstances of her former life, she declared that she was twice blessed because she had been recently taken out of the accursed jail of Babylon and was now about to be released from the wretched prison house of her body; when, perfectly conscious and sensible, she spoke in a way you would not expect of a woman about her own sins, the condemnation of eternal death, and the fearful judgment of God, and magnificently extolled the grace of Christ, and laid hold of it, with humility and trust, as a sacred anchor. I recall hearing her pour out those words as if I were still at her side watching and listening.[2] She did so not only clearly and distinctly but also with unusual vigor while she was breathing her last. Accordingly, on turning from that calamity and giving my attention to you, and seeing you succeed in your struggle to get the better of your sorrow, I was then just as amazed to find that when a man has the support of so many remedies of that sort he is brave in his grief.

I pass over other things that should be mentioned. I would only say that when Satan had prepared a confusing labyrinth for you out of the endless stock of scandals, you overcame them all in such a way that not only are you well qualified to give advice and encouragement to others, but also your example ought to put heart into those who are made of somewhat softer stuff and make you feel justified in walking with a quicker step. Certainly that fortress, the restraint of an even temperament, has been stoutly defended. You gave a conspicuous example of that in those other circumstances as well as in this one. Since you left behind in your native land those things that rush some people along the road of self-advancement, and hold others entranced by their allurements, you are not troubled in the slightest by a desire for them. It is thus quite evident that you do without those things with the same calm and troubled mind as once enabled you to renounce them without any difficulty.

Since I myself derive benefit from — and no ordinary delight in — this piety of yours, there can then be no cause for

2. See also Calvin to Madame de Cany, 30 April, 1549, CR, XIII, pp. 244-248.

wonder that I wish other people to share in it to some extent. For since you had been the prefect and the chief citizen of the city of my birth, I have recently been lamenting over you, as if you were a long way from Christ. Instead of that I now find that you are totally devoted to Christ, and I am claiming you as my very own and embracing you, so to speak, in the common bosom of the Church. However, my wish is that this little book might also be some sort of proof, to those who do not know you at all, of the love I bear you. For you yourself demand no pledge of it. There are indeed many bonds of true friendship binding us together, but no blood relationship or other tie can surpass our love. And so your unique brother has no difficulty with allowing you to be put on an equal footing with himself, because he realizes that he is loved in exactly the same way by you, like two things which balance each other perfectly.

164 Besides all that, seeing that a serious book appears because many people create a demand for it, my wish is that I could legitimately plead as an excuse the old saying, which I have quoted at the beginning of the book, "Soon enough done if well done."[3] But I am afraid that many people who, partly because of the comprehensive nature of the argument and partly because of the rather long delay, have been promising themselves some great work, will find the dashing of their hopes all the greater cause for offense when they discover matters that are thoroughly deserving of the richness, the splendor, the fervency of oratory, in a word, of all the flashes of eloquence, touched upon briefly, humbly, and dryly. To them I have no answer to give except that I have followed my own method, which I believed would be best. In so doing I do not ask that they agree with me but only that they might not refuse to allow me to disagree with them.

Goodbye, worthy Sir, and my most intimate brother in the Lord.

Dated at GENEVA, the tenth of July 1550, my birthday.

---

3. *Sat cito, si sat bene* (Cato to Hieronymus, Ep. 66, ch. 9). See also p. 8.

CONCERNING SCANDALS

*which, in our day, frighten away a great
many people, and are even the cause of
alienating some from the pure doctrine
of the gospel*

INTRODUCTION

"Scandal" Defined

After the Lord had pointed out many things to prove that he himself was the one who was to come for the salvation of the righteous, it was not without good reason that he ended by saying, "Blessed is he who shall find no occasion of stumbling in me" (Matt. 11:6; Luke 7:23). For, clearly, not only did he know that the proclamation of his gospel contained many things utterly abhorrent to human nature, but he also foresaw that Satan's cunning would be instrumental in raising obstacles of every kind, which would make it either detestable or suspect to the world. And, of course, what the Holy Spirit has made known about him is bound to be fulfilled, that he shall be "a stone of stumbling and a rock of offence,"[1] not that the true cause of offense lies in himself, as we shall soon see. But what does it mean? It means that what happens to him, indeed as if it were decreed, is that as often as he offers himself to men the majority stumble over him.[2] Whether or not this has ever occurred at any time in the past, we today are experiencing the truth of it from almost countless examples. The more fitting it is for us, then, to remind ourselves repeatedly of the warning which I have just quoted, that it might be firmly fixed in our minds, so that we may be delivered from the obstacles Satan puts in our way and also be turned away from him by that

---

1. *Lapis offensionis et petra scandali;* Isa. 8:14; I Pet. 2:8 (*RV*).
2. Lit. "strike against him" (*in eum impingant*). *Impingere* is generally translated "stumbling" throughout. [tr.]

blessing which Christ promises to his own. But how few there are who give any thought to this! On the contrary, how many, in fact, do we come across who, pleading the excuse of its scandals, either run away from the gospel as if it were some sort of danger or, having embraced it — even having made some progress in it — afterwards abandon the course! Accordingly, since I felt that there was no theme I would be more usefully engaged in handling, I have gladly undertaken the discussion of this one, especially since I pledged my word in this connection to certain worthy men, who are making constant demands for what I have promised, treating it like a debt. Perhaps it should have been done sooner, but since I was kept busy recently not only in writing other things which are just as necessary but also by many different duties, this will be a case of "soon enough done if well done."[3]

But before we come to the actual subject, we must see how this description — that he is "a stone of stumbling and a rock of offence" — can properly apply to Christ, when it is well known that he is the door to eternal life. Similarly, we must investigate how it can be that the teaching of the gospel, which is the one and only way to salvation, is constantly bound up with many scandals. This will become clearer if we start off with a *definition of a scandal.*

166   Since the way to live has been laid down for us by God, and we are obliged to him to follow it, it may be compared to a road or a race track. This gives rise to another metaphor: obstacles of all kinds, whether they divert us from the right direction, or keep us back by being in the way, or provide the means for making us fall, are called "scandals." It is certain that none of these things applies to Christ or his gospel. Christ's function is to lead us by the hand directly to the Father. Indeed, he is the light of the world by which we are guided to the Father, the way by which we come, the door by which we enter. It is of the nature of the gospel to remove all obstacles and to open up an easy entrance into the Kingdom of God for us. There is therefore nothing more out of keeping with Christ or the gospel than the name "scandal." There is absolutely not a shadow of doubt,

3. See close of Dedicatory Epistle, p. 4.

if we consider Christ in himself, that there is nothing more inconsistent with his nature than a scandal. And we are bound to hold the same view about the gospel. However, because of the perversity of men, what happens is that as soon as Christ comes on the scene, even at a distance, they are assailed on all sides by scandals; or, I should rather say, it is men themselves who run into the scandals. Christ is therefore "a rock of offence,"[4] not because he himself provides any occasion for stumbling, but because he is dragged in as the pretext for doing so. Thus, while the gospel teaches peace and concord, it is yet the cause of enormous disturbances because the ungodly seize upon it as an opportunity for fomenting trouble. But it would be extremely unjust to assign to Christ the blame and reproach that belong entirely to other people. And that is what Peter says: "Be yourselves built into a spiritual house" (I Pet. 2:5), [come to Him] "to that living stone, rejected indeed by men but chosen by God" (I Pet. 2:4).[5] "To you indeed, who believe, he is precious; but to those who do not believe he is the stone which the builders rejected, the stone on which they may stumble [offendant], the rock on which they may fall [impingant]."[6] For, observe, as Christ offers himself to all as the foundation, so they are built up into the temple of God. There is certainly no cause for offense about that. Why then do they stumble? Because instead of quietly giving their assent to him, in their obstinacy they rush upon him with blind fury. We realize, therefore, that such illwill or badness is rooted in human nature, so that what is accidental to Christ is just as normal as if it were of the very essence of his function.[7]

I now come to those who at one time embraced the gospel of Christ, and do not reject it now but yet wish to have it without scandals. I am dealing with Christians. Do they want Christ free from every scandal? Let them invent a new Christ for themselves! For he can be no other Son of God than the one made known in the Scriptures. Or let them at least change

4. Cf. pp. 8, 24.
5. The relative *qui* has no antecedent in Calvin's text. [tr.]
6. Cf. *RSV*. [tr.]
7. The last sentence begins the next paragraph in *B-N*, but seems preferable here. [tr.]

men's natures and make the whole world different! We listen to what the Scriptures tell us. This situation applies not only to the person of Christ but also to the whole of doctrine. It is not something temporary, but something that will continue in existence as long as the doctrine will be taught. Therefore, those people who today are rejecting the renascent teaching of the gospel merely on the pretext that they discover in it precisely what the prophets and apostles have predicted are being quite absurd! Nevertheless, they still wish to be regarded as Christians. What if they had been alive in the very first days of the gospel, when scandals of every kind were flowing in a constant stream from the gospel? How quick they would have been to put a lot of ground between themselves and Christ! How terrified they would have been in case they might have been mildly contaminated by any infection! If they say that they would not have done that in those days, why then are they so fastidious today? Why do they not recognize that the same characteristics are also to be found in Christ now? But a scandal is an odious and fearful thing to those of a modest disposition. Can anyone deny that? And I am not even saying that it is entirely our own affair whether we seek out scandals or not; let us avoid them because it is open for us to do so. But the fact is that the heart of a Christian ought to be so fortified that no matter what scandals burst on the scene he never yields ground or turns aside a hair's breadth from Christ. The man who is not equipped for perseverance like this, so as to overcome all scandals victoriously, does not yet understand the power of Christianity. But, of course, it is difficult to withstand scandals, especially when we are so soft and weak. I readily agree. But when we see the most holy name of Christ and his gospel being exposed to insult, it is certainly unreasonable to ask that we should be exempt from it. Accordingly, there are people who are today pretending that it is because of scandals that they are afraid to identify themselves with the pure teaching of the gospel which we profess, and, even more, shuddering at the thought of giving their assent to it. But I should like them all to be warned not to invent an idol for themselves instead of Christ. For it must remain a fixed principle that if we want to avoid all scandals, then we must at the same time refuse Christ, who

167

would not be the true Christ unless he were "a rock of offence." Now I know that there are four classes of men who are turned away from Christ by scandals, or who at least make them an excuse for their hostility to the gospel. A dread of scandals, which has its source in a certain natural modesty, holds many back from even venturing to sample the gospel. Others are lazier and more difficult to teach; but it is their stupidity rather than illwill that hampers them. But there are very many people who are intoxicated by pride and by a perverse view of his wisdom (from which they are far removed), and in their case their arrogance is the scandal. There are also those who carefully and maliciously catalogue all the scandals, and even invent many, and they do so with a hatred not so much of the scandals themselves but of the gospel, in order to bring it into disrepute in any possible way. And furthermore, when they do invent scandals they impudently twist all that springs from their illwill into the gospel.

One may see that the works of Sadoleto, Eck, Pighi, and Cochlaeus[8] are packed full of such misrepresentations. It is only right to deal more leniently with those of the first and second classes; the third and fourth must be repulsed more sharply. For when people reproach the Son of God with infamies for which they themselves are totally to blame, where does that spring from? Not from humanity I maintain — for what humanity can you expect from such cruel beasts?— but from a sense of shame. But we shall consider these things later.[9] I merely wished to point out at the beginning the kind of men I propose to deal with, so that my readers may gather from that what they ought to expect in this little book. Here the weak and the ignorant will discover what they can get to strengthen themselves for overcoming scandals. The ungodly will find what can avail for reversing their impious calumnies. What I am promising is something important; but I am confident that I shall be content if people judge me fairly. For it is too much to hope for that I shall cure the maladies of everybody. And I have already declared anyone guilty of great foolishness if he attempts to make

168

8. For a list of their works, see the note in *B-N*.
9. See, e.g., pp. 50 ff.

out that Christ is not a scandal to the ungodly. The scripture must be fulfilled which foretold that that would happen. And indeed I do not look for any other result from all the burning of the midnight oil that I have done, than that their fury will be roused more and more. But my concern is for the weak, for when their faith is shaky then it is our place to support it as with a sustaining hand. As far as those who are beyond hope are concerned, I shall be more than satisfied if I put a check on their impudence or at least prevent its poisonous influence from spreading further.

Three Classes of Scandals

No matter what subject is under consideration, making certain distinctions usually sheds a great deal of light on it. Accordingly, I shall discriminate briefly here between the main kinds of scandals which not only have been interfering with the progress of the gospel from the beginning but are also hindering it at the present day. Therefore, if you agree, we shall call some scandals "intrinsic," for they spring from the gospel itself, in men's opinion at any rate. Although others may originate elsewhere, they are nearly always connected with it. But others, which flow from unrelated and different sources we shall call "extrinsic" [adventitia].

In the first class are those whose origin is, as it were, part and parcel of the very doctrine of the gospel. Paul says that "the gospel is foolishness to the wise of this world" (I Cor. 1:18-20). And that is true, not only because its simplicity, which is popular and devoid of ostentation, is a laughing-stock to them, but also because it contains many things which, according to human standards, are irrational in the extreme — and ridiculous into the bargain! For the fact that the Son of God, who is life eternal, is declared to have put on our flesh and to have been a mortal man, the fact that we are said to have procured life by his death, righteousness by his condemnation, salvation by the curse he bore — all that is so greatly out of step with the common outlook of men that the more intelligent a man is the quicker will he be in repudiating it. Now, because the gospel deprives us of all credit for wisdom, virtue, and righteousness,

169

and leaves us with nothing but the utmost ignominy, it is of course inevitable that it causes serious offense. For such is the pride of our flesh that nobody is willing to let himself be stripped of those things which are the product of a deceitful imagination and of which we are all full. As a result there is the sharpest of clashes. People are also greatly offended by the severity of the demands for the denial of ourselves, the crucifying of the old man, contempt for the world, embracing of the cross. But even today experience itself is far more harsh when faith is put to the test by persecutions and other hardships. Add to these other things which, like those which we first mentioned, seem to be contradictory to human reason and completely absurd, and then indeed they give rise to thorny questions. These questions, in turn, create just as many scandals, that is to say, an infinite number. The doctrine of predestination[10] and similar doctrines are in that category.

The following scandals are in the second class and follow the appearance of the gospel on the scene. Disturbances and quarrels are the immediate consequence. The ungodliness which many had concealed before is now brought to light. A host of sects and strange and monstrous errors burst into life, and with their greater liberty many people grow insolent. Many of the teachers bring the doctrine itself into discredit by the example of their dissolute lives. The very ones who for a time seemed to be red-hot enthusiasts not only grow cold but are alienated from Christ in dreadful defection.[11] Yes, and Satan uses his wonderful tricks to make good and otherwise sincere teachers

10. B-N refers to works by Cochlaeus, Pighi, and Erasmus on free will; and by Johann Faber (1478-1511) on divine necessity; and to CR (opp. Calv.), VII, p. 247, lines 13 f.
11. B-N notes: "He is thinking of the Peasants' War and the disturbances of the Anabaptists (particularly those at Münster) and similar sects; he is perhaps also referring to the Quintinists." (See "Anabaptists," ODCC, p. 47.—tr.) For Quintinists (Quintinistae; French, Quintinistes) B-N cites: "Contre la secte phantastique et furieuse des Libertins qui se nomment spirituelz" (1545), CR (opp. Calv.), VII, pp. 165, 168, 200 ff.; and "Epistre contre un certain cordelier" (1547), CR, VII, pp. 361 ff. Calvin describes this monk (Cordelier) as a prisoner at Rouen, an instrument of the sect of the Libertines, and a supporter and defender of Quintin. At Tournai Quintin "renounced everything, alleging that he was a good Catholic, papal style. . . . On the scaffold he twice exhorted the people to take good care not to read the holy Scriptures." [tr.]

contend among themselves, so that, because of their weakness, he may attach some stigma to the doctrine. Furthermore, while the very newness of it all causes some people to take advantage of their freedom to be bolder, it is also normal for people who are faced with new things and are not yet firmly established, to pay closer attention to any mistakes. In this class, then, are these and similar things.

The third class partly consists of fictitious calumnies and partly springs from the ingratitude of men, when they bring forward various far-fetched accusations and spitefully and wrongly level them against the gospel in order to cause people to have nothing further to do with it. At the present time, when a great many of those who are regarded as believers are mixed up with men of a hostile and completely contrary point of view, and seek a way of cultivating their friendship, ambition is sweeping them off their feet like some sort of tempest so that they prefer to abandon the gospel rather than be cut off from ordinary life.

It has thus been worthwhile beginning with this distinction, seeing that I have to contend with so many and such different monsters; or, for this reason alone, that if infinity may not be enough to list the individual instances, the readers can refer to the classes.

170

PART I: THE FIRST CLASS OF SCANDALS: "INTRINSIC"

Scripture: Style

To begin then with the first class: proud men who are fond of ostentation are annoyed that in Scripture the Spirit employs popular, unpretentious language. Those who are also accustomed to what is splendid and elegant either reject or despise Scripture because its style is unpolished and free from embellishments. I am not willing to take up the aspect of the defense dealt with by others, that such contempt is born of ignorance, seeing that Moses and a great many of the prophets are just as accomplished in their own language as any of the Greek and Roman philosophers and orators who are read with the greatest admiration and approval.[1] For those who are sufficiently acquainted with Hebrew know that while Amos is just as much a prophet as Isaiah, and Jeremiah and David are on the same footing, yet their language is by no means on the same level of brilliance. What is more, the style of Jeremiah smacks of the townsman, while Amos's is redolent of the herdsman.[2] I readily concede that the sacred books, containing the whole of the heavenly philosophy as they do, are completely devoid not only of the word-pictures of the orators but also of the ordinary ornamentation which men of letters like. But these critics are far too fastidious, and that is why they have no discernment in these matters. Indeed, those who use this excuse to minimize

---

1. *B-N* refers to Augustine, *De doctrina christiana,* Bullinger, *De scripturae sanctae authoritate,* and Calvin, *Inst.,* I, viii, 2.
2. See p. 13, n. 11. The reference to *Inst.,* I, viii, 2 is appropriate here. [tr.]

the authority of Scripture are hostile and malicious in the extreme.

Paul acknowledges his lack of eloquence; indeed he goes further, and makes much of that lack and glories in it (I Cor. 2:1-5). Or is it the case that his teaching should, for that very reason, be all the more despised? No, on the contrary, he contends that where there is no brilliant oratory to blind people the heavenly wisdom blazes forth all the more powerfully. And indeed it is not until the fourth chapter of the First Epistle to the Corinthians[3] that he teaches anything about how faith is properly founded on the wisdom and power of the Holy Spirit only when men's minds are not captivated by elegance of speech and clever artifice. And anyone who has our experience regards that as the assured proof of faith. Of course, if the teaching of John or Paul had been embellished with all the colorfulness of a Demosthenes or a Cicero, perhaps it would have possessed more attractiveness for winning readers; but of its power for moving consciences and its value for gaining authority for itself not even one percent would be left. For in it the living God reveals himself in his majesty, so that all who read are forced to realize that it is God who is speaking to them, unless Satan deprives them of their wits. And that is why those who do not find Scripture to their taste because they do not find flowery language in it are dull in the extreme. But why should they find it attractive if God prefers to penetrate right to men's hearts rather than tickle their ears with delightful sounds? For Paul's words are also most apposite to our present purpose, that the treasure of the gospel is deposited in earthenware vessels so that the power of God might be all the more plainly seen in the weakness of men (II Cor. 4:7). We may take this as our principle, that no philosophers can argue so keenly as to be more powerful in persuading us, that no orators can influence us more forcibly with their fulminations, than Scripture with its plain, unvarnished style. For who does not see that it is due to the wonderful providence of God that the undisguised power of the Spirit may be all the more conspicuous in language of a humble kind? Those people wish to be captivated by the sweet tones of

171

3. Presumably I Cor. 4:20. [tr.]

eloquence. But the God who actually formed the tongue for men wishes to speak with us in stammering words. He stammers, but at the same time he uses tones of thunder; and what he utters is for the subduing of the minds of men with as lofty a dignity as if the most fluent of all the orators were bringing out all the choice words he had from an inner skill all his own. Paul teaches that in this way "spiritual things are adjusted to spiritual" (I Cor. 2:13),[4] and we see in perfect clarity how much the unadulterated truth of God effects by itself. Accordingly, men are too proud if aversion like that either keeps them from reading Scripture or weakens[5] the weight of its divine authority. But we may permit those people to keep the things that give them pleasure. If we ourselves have heard God speaking in our hearts, such plain, unpolished language will cause no offense to us, but rather may lead us on to a better contemplation of the majesty of the Spirit, which is conspicuous in it. For "the treasures of wisdom," which, Paul tells us, "are hidden in Christ" (Col. 2:3), must be brought to light in that way. And if anyone cares, he can find something about this subject in the first chapter of the *Institutes*, where I discuss the authority of Scripture.[6]

Central Dogmas of the Faith: Incarnation

Now, in order that we may proceed to find a remedy for scandals of the same class, shall we have to make a thorough examination of the dogmas which human reason does not find particularly attractive? Well, in that event the discussion would be endless; besides, such an examination can be carried out from my own and other people's lucubrations. And it would be a

172

4. Calvin has here, *spiritualia spiritualibus coaptari.* Commentary ad loc.: *spiritualibus spiritualia coaptantes. Vulg.* (WW), *spiritalibus spiritalia conparantes.* Cf. Commentary: "'to adjust or adapt' . . . suits Paul's context far better than 'to compare'. . . . He says therefore that he adjusts or adapts spiritual things to spiritual when he accommodates the words to the reality. In other words, he properly combines that heavenly wisdom of the Spirit with plainness of speech, and in such a way that it shows openly the very power of the Spirit himself." *The First Epistle of Paul the Apostle to the Corinthians* (Edinburgh, 1960), p. 60. [tr.]
5. Reading *elevat* for *elecat.* [tr.]
6. "He is referring to the edition of the Institutes of 1550, ch. 1:25; cf. the 1559 edition, I, viii, 1." — [B-N]. In *Beveridge,* Book I:7. [tr.]

waste of effort to bring forward scriptural testimonies for that purpose. For what would I be accomplishing were I to give a clear proof of the divinity of Christ to men like that? They will certainly fiercely reject anything I bring forward. What is more, the reason they reject the whole of Scripture is that whenever it does not happen to please them, they take up the attitude that it is absurd. Thus they appear to be intellectually superior in their own eyes only when they are laughing at our stupidity, because we accept with complete trust things that not only lack proof but are also incredible as far as human opinion goes. "Who is so ignorant," they ask, "as to allow himself to be persuaded about something for which he sees no reason?"

If I were to strive with such arguments as the human mind, acute as it is, can grasp, I should be exceedingly inept. For Paul acknowledges that our belief that Christ was God "manifested in the flesh" (I Tim. 3:16) is a mystery, far beyond the reach of all human perception. What then? If they plead any incongruity as an excuse, it will certainly be disposed of easily and in such a way that they will be forced to keep silence, unless they have a mind to bluster in their impudence. However, I shall not be able to do so without making them think that we are more stupid than any idiots you care to mention, seeing that we depend upon Scripture alone for convincing people about such great matters. That is why I shall address myself to those who are indeed troubled by scandals of that kind, but who are still curable.

To such people the only remedy I shall give is the one Paul prescribes, that they learn to become fools in this world in order to become capable of the heavenly wisdom (I Cor. 3:18). By "being fools" we do not mean being stupid; nor do we direct those who are learned in the liberal sciences to jettison their knowledge, and those who are gifted with quickness of mind to become dull, as if a man cannot be a Christian unless he is more like a beast than a man. The profession of Christianity requires us to be immature, not in our thinking, but in malice (I Cor. 14:20). But do not let anyone bring trust in his own mental resources or his learning into the school of Christ; do not let anyone be swollen with pride or full of distaste, and so be quick to reject what he is told, indeed even before he has sampled it. Provided that we show ourselves to be teachable we shall not be aware of any obstacle here.

But I am speaking only to those who rely on their own wisdom when I say that their arrogance is the scandal. How is that? Because the Son of God emptied himself to the extent of becoming your [*tuus*] brother, and uniting his eternal divinity to your mortal flesh, will that be an obstacle preventing you from yielding to him? Because God came down to you from his immense height, will you just for that very reason keep farther away from him? What if he should summon you up to the inaccessible sanctuaries of heaven? How would you endeavor to get to him at such a distance, when you take offense at his nearness? But you say it is like a fairy tale [*portenti*] to you to hear that God is mortal. But what else does that mean but that the immortal God has dwelt in our mortal flesh? For the truth   173
also declares that there is good reason for John's saying that glory has been seen in him, glory both appropriate to the Son of God (John 1:14) and offering clear evidence of his divinity. If you do not like to invent fairy tales, you would certainly not find one here. Our faith holds that God took a body that was subject to death. Here you are learning of a mystery for you to adore, not a fable for you to laugh at, or a monstrous thing for you to fear. Rather, put it down to your own ingratitude that wonder at such inestimable grace does not absorb all your hostile thoughts.

I know that these things are said to many people in vain. I am quite well aware of the way their derisive laughter pursues us, because we seek life in the death of Christ, grace in his curse, and justification in his condemnation. "Clearly," they protest, "it is like ice-cold water flowing out of a fiery furnace and light springing forth from darkness." They therefore conclude that nothing is too silly for us who hope that we shall be given life by a dead man, ask for pardon from a man who was condemned, derive the grace of God from a curse, and flee for refuge to a gallows as the one and only hope of eternal salvation. And, of course, when they laugh at our simplicity they seem to be exceedingly clever in their own eyes. But I maintain that they lack what is the principal thing in true wisdom, a sense of conscience. For what is wisdom, what is reasoning, what is discernment, when conscience has lost its power? And what is the root cause of their shrinking in horror like this from the fundamentals of the Christian religion except that they are completely intoxicated by Satan, with the result that they are not affected by any fear of God, or any thought of sin? I have already said that there is no other way by which we can attain to the wisdom of God than by becoming fools in this world. But the foundation of this humility, as of the whole of religion, is conscience and the fear of the Lord; if that is done away with, you may build your house in vain.

Therefore, anyone who wishes to overcome all the scandals that I have mentioned, without any trouble, only needs to look within himself, for as soon as he realizes his own wretched condition there will be a smooth, level road, not only for him to get to Christ but also for Christ to get to him. The voice of the prophet cries, "Prepare the way of the Lord" (Isa. 40:3).[7] And what reason is there for preparing it, except when men are driven to acknowledge their need, and to begin to have a longing for Christ, at whom they used to scoff in the days when they pleased themselves? In the same way let us also prepare the way for ourselves to Christ, and indeed that pious longing will be like horses and ships to us, enabling us to pass by all obstacles. For just as you need a cultivated and well-prepared mind in order to engage in the study of the higher disciplines, so you require a trained mind for the heavenly philosophy. For what taste is there for it where there is disgust? How can an entrance be effected when a total iron hardness has closed and barred the heart?

174 You may therefore talk about Christ, but it is to no purpose except with those who are genuinely humbled and realize how much they need a Redeemer, by whose mediation they may escape the destruction of eternal death. Therefore, any who do not wish to be deceived on their own responsibility, and to perish in their deception, should learn to begin here, so that they may realize that they have to deal with God, to whom reason must be surrendered once and for all. Let them keep before their eyes that judgment that even the angels must

7. Reading *viam* (with *Vulg.*) for *vias*. [tr.]

dread; let them think of how close their accuser, the Devil, is to them; let them listen to the evidence of their own conscience; let them not grow insensitive to the stings of sin; then there will be little danger of their finding anything scandalous in the death of Christ, of their being alarmed by the ignominy of the cross and, in short, of any other obstacle keeping them back.

One can find a very fine illustration of this situation in the woman of Samaria. All the time that Christ was speaking to her about the mystical drink of living water, she was chattering away pleasantly, but in a bantering way, sarcastic and somewhat bold, making light of it all. But after reproaching her for her adultery, he pricked her conscience. Immediately forgetting about her facetiousness, she reverently acknowledged the man whom she was previously so ready to torment with her witticisms to be a prophet (John 4:19). In the same way, those who think it absurd to seek for life by his death and to call the cursed cross the fountain of grace and salvation are offended by the fact that in Christ divinity is united with humanity in one person. Let us realize that those people are offended precisely because they have absolutely no fear of God, and so have no taste for spiritual teaching. Therefore, do not let their stupidity be a stumbling block for us, but rather let us be carried from the human nature of Christ to his divine glory, which changes all curious questions into admiration. Let us be directed from his death on the cross to his glorious resurrection that destroys all the disgrace of the cross. Let us pass from the weakness of the flesh to the power of the Spirit, which consumes all foolish thoughts. It is certain that Paul was imbued with such an outlook when he said, "I am not ashamed of the gospel of Christ, for it is the power of God unto salvation to those who believe" (Rom. 1:16). For with these words he is pointing out that it is precisely the people who do not grasp the saving power of the gospel who are ashamed of it. Moreover, it is capable of being comprehended only as the wrath of God revealed for our destruction. Now, will anyone be surprised that food is tasteless to those who have no palate? For anyone stupid enough to slumber peacefully on, undisturbed by any revelation of the wrath of God, is — as far as knowing Christ is concerned — no different from those who try to sample the flavor of something when their sense of taste has been destroyed. But we are not in the habit of wasting time on such people, in case any one of our own people might shrink from food on the grounds that it is rejected by them.

Human Wisdom and Righteousness

175

But now we come to another scandal which also has its source in doctrine, but one that is more potent and common. Because we are naturally pleased with ourselves and wish everything connected with ourselves to be given the highest possible value, all we have left to our name is a complete lack of all blessings as a result. For that is why the whole of human wisdom is condemned as foolishness, and human righteousness and virtue reduced to nothing. Of course, this seems such an intolerable thing to human pride that all those who have not yet learned to deny themselves grind their teeth in indignation. For men always desire to cling to anything of their own, and although under pressure they may yield to God to some extent, yet they simply cannot bear it that everything belonging to them be taken away at one fell swoop. To start with, they seem to be very wise in their own eyes, they are puffed up with confidence in their own virtue, and they think highly of their own righteousness. Afterwards, when they have been warned by God and they have also been convicted by experience playing its part, they realize that their wisdom is in fact untrustworthy and their virtue and righteousness defective; but it is quite impossible to bring them to believe that they are absolutely destitute of all wisdom and righteousness. But what else does this mean but sharing with God, as if a pact had been made?

But the gospel tells us that that light we imagine ourselves to have is nothing but darkness. In fact, so far from leaving us even a shred of righteousness, it pronounces all that we bring forward ourselves to be stinking and dirty in God's sight.[8] At this the worldly-wise will be burning with anger, and even the hypocrites will be in a rage. And this was the main reason why,

8. See, e.g., Isa. 64:6. [tr.]

22

at about the beginning of Christ's reign, a whole breed of philosophers, who were acting along with all the political authorities as if they were in a conspiracy with them, were so passionately opposed to the gospel. For they did not wish to be deprived of their own wisdom, for not only did they worship it as if it were an idol, but they also knew that they were held in the highest esteem because of it.

And how I wish that the ancient teachers had been less disturbed by the aversion of such men! For their anxiety to apply ointments to mollify them made them hand down to us a watered-down and degenerate theology. Origen, Tertullian, Cyprian, Basil, Chrysostom,[9] and all the others of the same class would never have spoken like that of their own accord. But in seeking a compromise to appease the wise of this world, or to avoid offending them, they have confused earthly things with heavenly. It was detestable, and contrary to common sense, to empty man completely. They devise something soothing,   176 which is more in accord with the outlook of the flesh; but at the same time the purity of the doctrine is polluted. Therefore, perhaps the best thing to do is to be bold and squeeze the sore itself, so that a diagnosis can be made based on the actual discharge. But there is nothing more obvious than that men have always been spurred on by fierce pride, making them declaim against the gospel. The same cause used to drive the Jews into a state of animal fury; for the evangelists, especially Luke and Paul, are witnesses that they were roused by it.[10] For they were struggling to defend their own righteousness, which was as insubstantial as smoke but yet seemed more precious to them than Christ. Both were rushing with violence and fury to attack the gospel, but the latter more fiercely, so that it might be plain to everyone that nobody surpasses hypocrites in virulence.

Christ himself speaks in general terms about this scandal when he says that "the sons of this age hate the light of the gospel, so that their evil deeds may not be exposed" (John 3:20).

9. See B-N for a list of works and a reference to *Inst.*, II, ii, 4.
10. This is somewhat obscure. Apart from Luke 4:28, there is no explicit reference, but cf. Acts 9:23; 13:50; 14:2, 19; 17:5; 18:12; II Cor. 11:24; John 7:23. [tr.]

For when the gospel is removed like the extinguishing of a light, the fallacious and feeble wisdom of the flesh shines in the darkness and gains control, and indeed a spurious sanctity spreads its proud wings everywhere. But as soon as the only Sun of Righteousness, Christ, bursts on the scene with the brightness of his gospel, those things which were previously filling its place of supreme honor not only vanish but are looked upon as filth. Naturally that gives rise to those tears! This is the fatal stumbling block to which Paul refers elsewhere, that "seeking to establish their own righteousness, they did not subject themselves to the righteousness of God" (Rom. 10:3). We also have experience of it in our own day. For you may discover few men, proudly convinced of their own wisdom, who are not stubborn enemies of the truth. Hypocrites are indeed hostile to the point of frenzy. And what other reason was there for Bunel[11] to abandon the gospel, except that, being a man who was born for ostentation, and who was excessively pleased with himself, he refused to be humbled against his will. I have cited the example of one man. How I wish that he did not have many like himself! But what are we to do? Let us leave them to stumble on "the stone of offence" (I Pet. 2:8),[12] so that the same thing which once happened to the Jews may befall them. "Seeking to establish their own righteousness," Paul says, "they did not subject themselves to the righteousness of God" (Rom. 10:3). So it comes about that they perish in their blindness. As for ourselves I say this, let us gladly offer ourselves, in our emptiness and nakedness to Christ, so that he may fill us with his blessings, and clothe us with his glory, and this kind of scandal will be abolished.

Difficulties in Scripture

In truth I should be attempting something like emptying the sea if I wished to examine and enumerate one by one all the scan-

11. *Bunellus. B-N* refer to A. Samouillan, *De Petro Brunello* [*sic*] (Paris, 1891), ch. 4. Calvin's reference to him here is quoted in Peter Bayle, "Peter Bunel," *The Dictionary Historical and Critical* (ET, 2nd ed., London, 1735), p. 201. "When he was young he had taken some liking to the doctrine of the Reformed. . . . Some Catholics believed that Bunel retained some tincture of Protestantism to his death" (at the age of 47).
12. *In lapidem offensionis*; pp. 8 and 9 above.

dals which wretched men devise for their own destruction out of the teaching of Scripture. For it is not simply a matter of their making a blind assault if they run up against some difficulty, but, having freely given their minds to the matter, they become agitated by all the rough features, as if their one satisfaction in life lay in tormenting their minds with thorny questions. For they carefully note anything that shows the slightest sign of being irrational, and criticize it sharply, so as not to give the impression that they can be made to believe all that easily. If there is also any appearance of disagreement and contradiction in several Scripture passages, they seize on it eagerly, and by collecting all the examples of that kind, they make a great fuss about their own shrewdness. Besides, men like that are afflicted by an almost incurable disease. For although it makes them feel ashamed not to know something, yet they cannot bear to learn anything. But because by their boasting they upset people who are very often simple but otherwise quite capable of being taught, it was necessary to touch on that part of scandals, not that they can be disposed of in a few words, when even a lengthy book would not be enough to deal with them. But, in the first place, all of us need to take heed, so that in reading Scripture we keep to the way the Spirit of God points out to us; and for those who are aspiring to come close to Christ, it will certainly be a plain, consistent way. In the second place, we should not have a desire to be or to appear clever by complicating difficult questions. Finally, if we find something that is strange and beyond our understanding, do not let us be quick to reject it. That many people let their ignorance develop immediately into aversion is a fault deserving severe censure. But, in fact, the man who says that any divine pronouncements which he himself does not understand are not God's oracles at all has little reverence for God. For what is that but assessing the infinite wisdom of God by the small measure of our mind? It is like using a finger to measure the whole world! But if we acknowledge that Scripture has come forth from God, then we should not be surprised if it contains many things that are beyond our understanding. To sum up, in religion this is the way and order of wisdom, to strive earnestly for a right understanding with the obedience of faith.

177

The Cross and Suffering

In the parable comparing the gospel with sowing (Matt. 13:3-9), our Lord speaks about the scandal, which has its origin in the harshness or vexation of the cross and the austerity of the teaching. For he compares those who defect[13] when persecution assails them to seed that has sprung up without any root; and those in whom the teaching is veritably choked by the cares of this world to the seed sprouting among thorns, which prevent its coming to fruitful maturity. These scandals differ to some extent, but for the sake of brevity I am classifying them together. We hear Christ commanding all his disciples that each one is to take up his own cross (Matt. 10:38; 16:24). We hear him exhorting them to submit to hatred, dangers, and reproaches of all sorts for his name's sake (Matt. 10:22). We hear his warning that it is inevitable for us to be hated by unbelievers and beset by afflictions in this world (Matt. 24:9). We hear him calling "blessed" all those who endure persecution for the sake of the truth (Matt. 5:10). To flesh and blood this is the greatest of scandals, for it is natural for all of us to dread the cross. Therefore, for this reason many draw back who would otherwise gladly embrace the Son of God, if they could separate him from the cross. But where does this scandal come from but our own softness? Christ bids us die with him in order that we may be sharers in his life (II Cor. 5:14f.). He wishes to lead us to his glory by means of "the fellowship of his sufferings" (Phil. 3:10). That is not an unfair demand, if we had any fairness in us. But many would desire to have the Christ of glory, suppressing all mention of the cross. That simply cannot be done. And not even content with that, they transfer the blame which lies with themselves to the teaching itself. Thus the people of Capernaum once protested that one of Christ's sayings was hard (John 6:60), when the hardness was not in what he said but in themselves. Are we surprised if the Son of God wishes to have disciples who are discerning and not soft or effeminate? Are we surprised if he wishes them to wear his badges, or orders them to fight under his standard?

178

13. *Deficiunt. Vulg.* (Matt. 13:21), *scandalizatur;* Greek, *skandalizetai; RV,* "stumble." [tr.]

Denial of the Flesh

To this malady is related that other one which I have mentioned. For the denial of the flesh is such an irksome thing that it frightens many from coming into the school of Christ, and drives out others who have made a start in it. They may very well put up with a discussion of the question of original sin and the common faults of nature. They gladly concede that the grace of God and the benefits of Christ are to be honored with their praises, but when it comes to a question of curing the diseases of individuals, they are obstinate in their rejection of a drastic medicine. So one may discover many people who had been delighted with the gospel when they first tasted it but who began to find it an extremely bitter thing as soon as it pricked their consciences. Of course, since the word of God is "a two-edged sword," and its functions are not only to lay bare and condemn obvious faults[14] but also to penetrate to the secret depths of our hearts, to pierce through all the innermost parts of our being, and to distinguish between our intentions and thoughts (Heb. 4:12),[15] and finally, to present the whole man as an offering to God — those men are not willing to have their wounds touched. People ask to be left with freedom, some to fly into a fury, others to plunder, others to indulge in fornication, and still others to indulge in dissipation. They all wish to follow the course of their own vanity with impunity. Is there any reason, therefore, to wonder if they turn their backs on Christ?

But suppose someone may say, "This makes clear what the scandal is; it does not remove it." My reply to that is that the disease had to be made known in order that a remedy might at last be procured. Our minds need their weakness to be corrected, instead of their encouraging the fault of looking for excuses, which do nothing at all to help us. But that is a difficult business, and who would deny it? Yet we must struggle, and we must do so not in our strength but in that of Christ, who not only commits us to battle but also equips us with the arms necessary for victory. Oh! if we were to grasp the meaning of

---

14. *Vitia. B-N:* "1550 has, wrongly, *via.*"
15. *Discernere inter affectus et cogitationes.* Cf. *Vulg., discretor cogitationum et intentionum cordis.* [tr.]

27

179 "Blessed are those who are persecuted for righteousness' sake" (Matt. 5:10), how easy it would be for us to surmount not merely this particular stumbling block but whatever the world and the flesh inflict upon us! To you [*tibi*] persecution is so grievous that you are retreating from Christ. Why? You have no idea how valuable Christ is. Concern about this present life is dragging you away from him, doubtless because you have no taste for the life to come. Avarice is burning you up, doubtless because you do not yet grasp what the true riches are. You are intoxicated with ambition because, clearly, you have not yet learned to glory in the Lord. Gluttony, sexual lust, displays, or other empty delights lure you because you are still ignorant of that sweetness[16] which the prophet declares is "laid up for them that fear" God (Ps. 31:20).[17] Finally, it is not surprising that few Christians are in fact to be found, seeing that there are few who have come to realize that Christ is so precious that they regard everything else as so much filth. There will be a place for exhortations elsewhere. Here scandals must be dealt with in such a way that it may be quite clear to what they must properly be attributed.

The Poor State of the Church

But why am I discussing the private afflictions of the individual, when the situation of the Church Universal contains in itself far greater grounds for offense? In the first place, it never shines with that splendor, which would enable the minds of men to recognize the Kingdom of God. Secondly, if ever it succeeds in rising to some modest position, soon afterwards it is either crushed by the violence of tyrants or collapses of its own accord, so that that situation lasts only for a short time. Throughout the centuries this has meant that men in their pride either despised the true religion or even treated it with contempt and abuse. We see the insolent way Cicero[18] scoffs at the law of God, because circumstances were by no means favorable to the Jews. From this man alone one can form an estimate of

---

16. *Suavitatem*. Cf. *Vulg.*, *multitudo dulcedinis; EVV*, "goodness," following Hebrew. [tr.]
17. *B-N* with Hebrew. Cf. *LXX*, Ps. 30:19; *Vulg.*, Ps. 30:20; *EVV*, Ps. 31:19. [tr.]
18. Cicero, *Pro L. Flacco*, XXVIII, 69. [*B-N*]

them all. And so as not to digress further, what is the reason why many people are shrinking today from making a genuine profession of the gospel, except that they see that we are few in number and also have very little authority — indeed no power — while they are admirers of all the contrary things on the opposite side? And certainly, as things are today, there is no need to be surprised if such a deformed state of the Church is frightening them away, but the brilliance that shines in its opponents is blinding their eyes.

In truth, the only people who stumble on this stone and the only people kept back by this stumbling block are those who do not discern the spiritual Kingdom of Christ. For those who allow neither the stable in which Christ was born nor the cross on which he hung to prevent them from giving honor to the King himself, will not in the least despise the poor condition of his Church. Indeed, they all confess with their lips, and the confession needs to be made, that it is particularly reasonable that in the form of the Church the living image of Christ should appear as in a mirror. And when Paul speaks about the similarity between head and members in bearing the cross (Rom. 8:17), they are all in agreement. When he says that we ought to die with him in order that we may be sharers in his life (II Tim. 2:11), nobody cries out in protest. When the whole of Scripture compares this present life to a stern warfare and teaches that it is filled with many different struggles, they nod their assent that it is all true and correct. Therefore, the name "Church Militant" is so commonplace and trite that it echoes even on the lips of children. But when it comes to the point of decision, they seem to have forgotten all those things and run away from the image of Christ as though it were some strange monster. 180

But supposing they were to get what they long for, a church well-favored in every way, flourishing with wealth and influence, enjoying unbroken peace — in short, lacking nothing to make its circumstances prosperous and most desirable — will it not have the appearance of an earthly power? Accordingly, the spiritual Kingdom of Christ will have to be sought elsewhere; and furthermore, the Church will be cut off from its head. However, let us remember that the outward aspect of the Church is so contemptible that its beauty may shine within;

that it is so tossed about on earth that it may have a permanent dwelling-place in heaven; that it lies so wounded and broken in the eyes of the world that it may stand, vigorous and whole, in the presence of God and his angels; that it is so wretched in the flesh that its happiness may nevertheless be restored for it in the spirit. In the same way, when Christ lay despised in a stable, multitudes of angels were singing his excellence; the star in the heavens was giving proof of his glory; and the magi from a far-off land realized his significance. When he was hungry in the wilderness and when he was contending with the taunts of Satan to the point of sweating blood, the angels were once again ministering to him [Mark 1:13; Luke 22:43f.]. When he was just about to be fettered he drove back his enemies with his words alone [John 18:6]. When the sun failed, it was proclaiming him — hanging on the cross — King of the world; and the open tombs were acknowledging him Lord of death and life [Matt. 27:45, 52f.]. Now, if we see Christ in his own body tormented by the insults of the wicked in their arrogance, crushed by cruel tyranny, exposed to derisive behavior, violently dragged this way and that, do not let us be frightened by any of those things, as if they were unusual. On the contrary, let us be convinced that the Church has been ordained for this purpose, that as long as it is a sojourner in the world it is to wage war under the perpetual cross.

God's Power Seen in the Church's Troubles

Now, if we were skillful and fair interpreters of the works of God, the very thing that we seize upon as an excuse for a stumbling block would be the source of the greatest encouragement to us. For the Church's condition is very often calamitous and always unstable; indeed it is being continually tossed about by many different tempests just as in a stormy sea. In the first place, the Lord is showing us in that a clear example of his marvelous providence; and secondly, it provides a useful and indeed necessary exercise for putting our faith and our patience to the test. If the Church had been so established and equipped with aids of every kind that it glittered with its riches, it would be no different from any worldly power; and indeed, no one would doubt that it is ruled according to human standards if it had persisted to this very day in the accustomed manner. But when we see that its life has nevertheless endured for so many generations as if through innumerable deaths, we are bound to conclude that it was preserved by the providence of God. Other circumstances make this power of God still clearer to us, because when it was attacked on all sides by deadly perils, which could have overwhelmed it time and again — with almost the whole world reluctant and glittering in contrast — it always escaped as if from shipwreck. I am not speaking about anything that anyone who is willing to look at the historical records of all the past ages may not easily get to know for himself. It is an ancient complaint of the Church that "from her youth she was attacked again and again," and encountered such hostile unbelievers that they "ploughed upon her back, and made long their furrows" (Ps. 129:1-3).[19] With these words the Spirit of God wished to revive the godly when they were groaning under the severest of hardships, so that, by glancing at every period of time from the beginning of the world, they might realize that the Church has always overcome by suffering. We ought to pay attention to this thought, so that if ever the state of things in our own time causes us distress, the recollection of those things, which our fathers experienced long ago, may give us fresh heart. It will thus be useful to give a brief description of all the ages, so that as often as the situation and the need demand, each of us may use that to place before his own eyes examples that are suitable for the relieving of our own afflictions.

181

Digression: Origin of the Church's Troubles

But before I proceed any further, it is worthwhile noting what is the origin of such numerous and varied changes by which the Church of God is repeatedly disturbed and, so to speak, whirled about. Certainly an understanding of this problem is not to be sought in irrelevant or obscure conjectures,

19. With Hebrew; LXX, Ps. 128:1-3. Cf. *Vulg.*, *prolongaverunt iniquitatem suam; LXX, emakrunan tēn anomian autōn.* With Heb. and *EVV,* Calvin reads "their furrows." [tr.]

since men's constant revolts from God are what have interrupted the otherwise constant and unimpeded course of his grace. One can observe that truth from almost the very beginning of the world itself. When Moses speaks about Seth and his son Enosh, he recounts that "at that time men began to call upon the name of the Lord" (Gen. 4:26), and we understand from that that the true worship of God (which had lapsed to some extent with Cain's accursed descendants) had been restored once again to thrive and flourish in the world. But scarcely eight generations passed before all their descendants, whom God had set apart to be his own sons, rushed into every kind of sin, so that in the flood they destroyed, along with themselves, the whole world, which they had polluted by their disgraceful conduct.

When the Church had been reduced to eight souls, it at least seemed to be so purified that that scanty seed which was left would produce from itself nothing but genuine holiness. But soon it was reduced by a quarter.[20] The descendants of Japhet also disappeared a little later. Only the family of Shem was left, and not long afterwards it also became so degenerate that a large part of it was deservedly renounced by God. After the descendants of Abraham were brought out of Egypt with wonderful power and crossed the Red Sea, they proceeded toward the inheritance promised them. Who would not predict from such auspices a perpetual state of blessedness? But those very people, in whose deliverance God had given such a remarkable example of his power, knew no limit to their sin, until they were all destroyed by horrible means in the wilderness. Their children at last entered on their possession; but for almost six[21] generations their land knew no stability, because they were constantly disturbing it by their treacherous fickleness. However, the Lord did quite frequently restore them to a tolerable form of life. All the same, neither the memory of their first deliverance, nor the rods so often used to punish them, nor an awareness of present punishments, nor the indulgence frequently shown them, could restrain them from throwing off God's yoke and bringing fresh disasters on themselves.

182

20. Gen. 9:25, the curse on Ham. [tr.]
21. "1550 has, wrongly, six hundred." [B-N]

Moses had predicted that this would happen; they would be "fat and well fed" and disobedient (Deut. 32:15). But the actual state of affairs goes far beyond that. What is the history of the Jews but a record of one rebellion after another? Therefore, if any are offended by the many different disturbances to which they see the Church exposed in this world, let them take a look in that mirror, and they will cease to be amazed that those who come and go with so much inconstancy of faith in the presence of God do not have a fixed abode on the earth. When David's kingdom was set up, a regular plan for a sound and lasting state seemed more assured. But for three days, pestilence, that lamentable catastrophe, raged in a strange manner through the land and left little of their good fortune (II Sam. 24:13-17). Immediately after the death of Solomon the body of the people was itself split. From then on the mangled parts were continually attacking each other, and each kingdom also suffered the torment and misery of external wars. Shall we say that they were being driven by their fate? Let us rather say that they themselves urged on and hastened the punishment of God by their sins. For they appeared to be absolutely innocent when David carried out the census, because that was the personal offense of one man; yet the sacred history relates that God's anger burned against them all (II Sam. 24:15).

At last there came that greater change, not far removed from ultimate destruction, when the whole nation was carried off into exile in Babylon. But surely if their desperate stubbornness had not driven them headlong, they would never have come to this calamity. The return after seventy years was like a second birth for them. But as soon as they were back home they forgot such a great blessing, and once again fell away into various corrupt practices. Some defiled themselves by marrying heathen (Ezra 9:1ff.); others most shamefully defrauded God of tithes and first-fruits (Neh. 5:1ff.);[22] while the building of the temple was postponed and neglected, others were wholly taken up with furnishing palaces and incurred enormous expense (Hag. 1:2-4). Such base ingratitude went beyond the score, and all will acknowledge that it ought not to have gone unpunished.

22. So B-N, but rather Neh. 10:32-39; 13:10-14. [tr.]

183   Therefore, the fact that they no longer enjoyed peaceful and favorable conditions must be put down to their own fault.

Indeed, after Christ, the source of peace and every blessing, became known to the world, men would really have found out how assured and well-founded is the happiness of his eternal Kingdom, if they had allowed him to remain in their midst. But never has the world been shaken by more violent storms of wars, never has it been submerged by the filthy waters of misfortunes so varied and so deep. The cause does not lie hidden in such obscurity that it cannot easily be found out by investigation. Christ was born; everywhere there was peace and great tranquility. About forty years later his gospel was being spread through many different parts of the world. After it had thundered far and wide, like a sudden turn of fortune's wheel, turbulent conditions existed everywhere. What was the reason for such a change except that, after his gospel had been despised and rejected, God was punishing such great ingratitude, and it was all the more obvious because he did it so quickly? Therefore, when infamous men were putting the blame for any disasters that arose in those days on the name of Christ, it was an easy matter for the pious teachers of the Church to put an end to their calumnies, worthless as they were.[23]

What then? Since kings and nations rejected the peace God offered them, was it not just that they should fight among themselves, so as to perish from the wounds they inflicted on each other? And can those who refuse to submit themselves to God retain any sort of order in their way of life? I am not so much referring to avowed enemies — those stubborn in their resistance to the sound teaching of piety — but to those who actually gave their allegiance to Christ, when I say that many of them gave to Christ a kiss that was cold and contemptuous, while others gave him one that was treacherous and insincere. Those who are offended by examples of God's severity in this connection might be just as eager to find fault with him for doing nothing! But unless we are reluctant to open our eyes we shall see[24] that in the case of all those to whom God has ever

---

23. References are given in B-N to Tertullian, *Apology*, 40 ff.; Augustine, *De civitate Dei*, I, i, 7.
24. "1550 lacks *perspiciemus*, added here." [B-N]

revealed himself, it was only their own fault that when they placed their happiness in their own safety it was[25] short-lived and slight; and we shall also see that they had nobody to blame but themselves for their own wretchedness. We know that Jerusalem was the source from which salvation streamed right to the farthest corners of the earth. In all their predictions the prophets used to promise complete restoration to her with the coming of Christ.[26] But it fell out far differently. For she came to retain not even a pale shadow of her former greatness, and soon afterwards she not only lost what was left to her but she was utterly destroyed and reduced to an empty wasteland. Why does nobody take pains to inquire into the reason for such an unnatural catastrophe, except that the desperate disobedience of the people proclaims in no uncertain voice that it was the cause? Never was Rome afflicted within a short space of time by such severe disasters, as after the gospel had reached it. How did it come about that, in the very city where for so long the unbridled passion of the common people was rampant, where nefarious factions and, finally, cruel tyrants held sway, the Kingdom of Christ could not have a secure throne? It is surely that when God brought forward the gospel, the ultimate cure for so many deadly diseases, they rejected it in their pride, and like men devoted to destruction they continued to rush from bad to worse.

184

The same thing can also be observed in our own time. A few years after the remarkable beginnings of the reborn Church had appeared, we then saw them collapse back into ruins. But before the Lord inflicted this punishment upon us, we saw many filthy profanations of the gospel on all sides, so that we are to wonder, not so much that this sudden overthrow of events took place, but at his great patience in putting up with the prodigious enormities of our time. When so many thousands renounced the Pope and eagerly — so it seemed — came over to the side of the gospel, I may tell you how few there were who repented of their erroneous ways. On the contrary, did not the majority make it clear that, having shaken off the

25. "1550 reads, wrongly, *constitueret*; amended here to *consisteret*." [B-N]
26. Isa. 60, 62; Jer. 33:16f.; Ezek. 43-47; Mic. 4; 7:7-11; Zeph. (Latin "Zed") 3:16-20; Zech. 6:9-15; 8; 9:9f.; 14:12-21.

yoke of superstitious practices, they had more freedom to abandon themselves to licentiousness of every kind? Therefore, although they acknowledged that the teaching of the gospel is the truth, how few submitted to its discipline! What else were they doing but, so to speak, treading under their feet the incalculable treasure of the gospel? And indeed the harshness of the punishment that followed such impious contempt ought to remind us of its value rather than produce absurd ideas in our minds about accidental disturbances of the Church. Yes, and when our ingratitude is so great, it is a wonder that anything still remains of the work which God began.

The Church's History of Suffering: The Old Testament

I now come back to the theme, from which I have digressed a little, that God is known better as the preserver of his Church, because it has always been miserably harassed, than if it had flourished peacefully and happily in the most favorable of circumstances. According to Moses, when the name of God began to be invoked among the family of Seth, there is no doubt that Cain's descendants, being superior in numbers and more presumptuous, vaunted themselves in a most savage way against those people, who were not only few in number but also gentle [Gen. 4:17-26]. Therefore, could such lambs have continued to remain safe among wolves if they had not been protected by the supporting hand of God? Then as time continued to pass, violence, along with wickedness, also saw to the harming of the ungodly.[27] Or shall we say that those who were living like subjugated people among such hostile beasts remained human? If not, perhaps someone may imagine that the giants were kept within bounds so that they spared the pious people, who were subject to them and by whom they came to know themselves as a detestable, adulterous race.

Finally, one man and his tiny family were left. Having been commanded by the Lord to build an ark (Gen. 6:14) for the

27. *Improbis*; see Gen. 6:1-6. The suggestion is that "the sons of God" were the descendants of Seth, and were "pious" until corrupted by the Nephilim. [tr.]

continuous period of one hundred and twenty years, he   185
brought down on himself the fury of those who were raving like
madmen against God (Gen. 6:13). [28] For he gave a plain warning
to everyone of the threatening disaster when he procured a new
place of refuge for his life (Heb. 11:7). How often do we think of
him, when he was provoked by the insults and wickedness of
those people, as contending fiercely for the righteousness of
God? Indeed, when the ferocity of enemies was so great, would
he not have had to undergo just as many deaths if the hand of
God had not snatched him away? Besides, if he had not been
undergirded by the power of heaven, he would have perished
of his own accord a thousand times every year. Finally, a greater
and diviner miracle followed in the ark: because he was deprived of air and atmosphere, there was no life for him, only
the grave; because he did not have the breath of life to breathe,
there was only deadly suffocation; in a word, he could survive
on the earth only by separating himself from the whole world.

When God had renewed the world, so to speak, after it
emerged from the flood, there followed not long afterwards a far
worse and more destructive flood, because all the nations were
in the grip of wickedness (Gen. 11:1-9). And this one did not
last for ten months, but by raging through the long course of
years it gathered force, so that the family of Shem itself, the
more sacred personal possession of God, would also have been
nearly engulfed had it not been that in the midst of the vast
flood Melchizedek, along with a few others, kept up the pure
worship of God and remained upright and blameless. And that
was the one and only reason why that man emerged (Gen.
14:18). [29] It was surely to keep Abraham safe that God brought
him out of the deep whirlpool of idolatry (Josh. 24:2f.). Further,
having been brought into the land that was destined to be his
inheritance, he was merely a sojourner in it, so that on one
occasion he was forced into a dispute about water (Gen.
21:25f.), and on another was driven away by famine to another
land (Gen. 12:10). In order to escape death when he was dealing

---

28. Gen. 6:13. [B-N] Rather 6:3, from which Calvin took the view that the
human race would exist only for another 120 years, during which Noah
worked on the ark. See Matt. 24:38; Luke 17:27; Heb. 11:7. [tr.]
29. Lit., "for swimming out." [tr.]

with two kings, he found no other remedy than to put out his wife, dearer to him than life, like a piece of booty (Gen. 12:11ff.; Gen. 20). His son and grandson went through similar and even severer troubles, contending daily with cruel and barbarous men as with wild beasts, and not without risk to their lives. If anyone does not see plain evidence of the hand of God in upholding and preserving them, then he must surely be as blind as a bat.

David is, of course, perfectly justified in honoring that protection of God which had kept them safe with a remarkable utterance, when he says that "kings were not allowed to hurt the Lord's anointed ones, and to do harm to his prophets" (Ps. 105:15). They were few in number; they were aliens and unknown; unsettled, they wandered about from place to place; on all sides they were surrounded by treacherous and savage peoples, and every single moment brought some fresh crisis with it. Indeed, I grant that this has been a contemptible, almost disgraceful spectacle in the eyes of proud men; but as I have already said,[30] in this despicable situation God's extraordinary guardianship was better reflected, just as in a mirror. Furthermore, one may see more clearly that it was not a case of the Church being pulled out of one flood on a single occasion, but that it continued to remain afloat when one inundation of evil followed another all down the long course of the ages.

186

There followed the bondage of Egypt, and that would have resulted in nothing short of their complete shipwreck had not God come to their aid in due course. I make no mention of how irksome and unjust their bondage was, because having been made to undertake mean and filthy tasks and to undergo frightful hardships, they were struggling just to keep alive. But when Pharaoh ordered the complete destruction of the male children, who would not have said that that was the last straw? The midwives lied so as not to appear as accessories to the cruelty of the king (Exod. 1:19). And finally the deliverer of the people, Moses himself, was put into an ark of rushes and exposed by the bank of the river (Exod. 2:3). Now it seemed that the salvation of all of them was to be despaired of, and their name was to be completely wiped out. We shall therefore judge how remark-

30. See pp. 36-37.

able a miracle of God it was that those who could have been destroyed time and time again not only remained intact but made those remarkable increases which are referred to by Moses [Exod. 1:7, 12, 20].

Indeed, it is in this matter of pondering the works of God that the depravity of men reveals itself in all its malignancy. For if men hear of something which God has brought about for the safety of the Church and which, in their opinion, is too great, they dismiss it as fabulous. Anything that is commonplace and not in any way unusual they haughtily dismiss as having happened by chance, or at least by human agency. But if the condition of the Church is not favorable or happy, they seize upon this straightaway as grounds for a scandal. Accordingly, Moses' accounts that such burdensome and degrading work among bricks was inflicted on the wretched Jews as if they were beasts of burden (Exod. 1:14), that their male children were doomed to be slaughtered at birth (Exod. 1:22), that a vulgar mob fled in secret with the jewelry[31] they had hastily acquired (Exod. 12:35f.), all seem to very many people to be out of keeping with the glory of the Church. Moses reports that Jacob, with his family, was courteously received by Pharaoh, that he was treated with kindness, and that he was endowed with wealth in cattle; but they consider these things to be simply a matter of good luck. One family is said to have grown into an enormous people in a fairly short period of time (Exod. 1:6f.), and the same Moses teaches that so many portents were given by God in order that he might redeem the hopeless and desperate Israelites (Exod. 7-12). But because these things go beyond credibility, men mock at them as if they were fictitious. Therefore, so that we might bring fresh minds to the contemplation of the works of God, they must first be cleansed of this innate perverseness of ours.

Examples of God's providence in preserving the Church deserve to be distinguished by great brilliance of language, but so that I may not appear to be writing a history (because after all that is not our present purpose), it is enough for me to touch

---

31. With *EVV.* Lit. "vessels," *vasis.* Cf. *Vulg.,* Exod. 12:35, *vasa argentea et aurea.* Hebrew, "vessels of silver." [tr.]

187 upon them lightly, as if in passing. However, the plan of this work does not allow me to mention even the tenth part. Indeed, there is no great need for that, provided my readers grasp this one thing that I want them to know: the more the Church has been crushed beneath the cross, the more clearly has the power of God shown itself in raising it up again. After the people entered the land of Canaan, their unbelief prevented them from possessing it in peace, undisturbed by enemies. Thereafter they were constantly assailed by invading enemies. Then when their forces had been crushed and broken, they were exposed to plunder and pillage. Moreover, the people rather often changed their masters [Judg. 3:8, 14; 4:2; 6:1, etc.] who, however, eagerly conspired to destroy them so that the wonder is that they came through so many terrible and close disasters. Certainly after the capture of the ark of the Lord (I Sam. 4:11) they were not even a finger's breadth from final despair, for that took the heart out of them more than the severe defeat. Nearly all the flower of their manhood perished; routed and scattered, they gave themselves over to weeping and lamentation. Not even when they sought a remedy because of the severity of the misfortunes was any alleviation given at first; it was later that salvation, exceeding their expectation, suddenly dawned from heaven. After Saul was killed, there was the threat of similar destruction (I Sam. 31), but David quickly restored the collapsing situation (II Sam. 2ff.). If there had been a continuous period of peace and prosperity, the extraordinary blessedness of that people could certainly have been extolled in grander eulogies; but the deliverances so marvelously wrought by God would not have been recognized in the same way.

When the ten tribes later cut themselves off from the body of the people (I Kgs. 12), such a separation — when they were surrounded by many enemies eagerly on the lookout for a chance to do them mischief — seemed to threaten them with immediate destruction. The Israelites afterwards lapsed into alien religious rites (I Kgs. 12:28ff.). They were therefore disinherited in a measure from the family of God. Nobody would imagine that the remaining part, which is regarded as the Church of God, would last for long. And certainly that people was often forced to such a point of necessity that—despairing of salvation—it waited, terrified, for some final extremity. In the time of Ahaz, two very powerful kings had attacked even Jerusalem itself, and the whole region was already in flames, as if a double fire had swept through it. Ahaz himself was paralyzed with fright and would easily have gone down before the first insults of his enemies.[32] Such a great fire was suddenly put out without any human agency, and even the smoke was dispersed. In that deliverance, was not the glory of God pouring itself out in full splendor? However, when Sennacherib had occupied the kingdom, which was stripped of defenses, he fell with fury upon the city, then in a state of confusion and quite unprepared for resistance. King Hezekiah was virtually a prisoner. There was no way of escape; there were no resources within the city and no assistance from any other source (Isa. 37:1ff.). When the enemy, in all his pride and arrogance, was removed to another place soon afterwards, did not this unexpected change then bear out the truth of what Isaiah had predicted — that it would be an easy matter for God either to tame or put a check on that ferocious beast (Isa. 37:29). But when Sennacherib came back a little later, flushed by a new victory, the Lord produced quite a different example of his grace and power in raising the siege. For he did not summon Sennacherib away by human agents, or smash his attacks by orthodox means, and break off indecisive engagements; he deprived him of his army in a single night by a strange slaughter at the hand of his angel, and then destroyed him when he was defenseless and despoiled after an ignominious flight, far from Judah, which during his victorious days he had held with enormous forces (Isa. 37:36-38). This one incident is certainly a splendid lesson: sometimes there is nothing more beneficial for the Church than being beset by extreme difficulties, so that it may learn to ascribe its escape — safe and sound — to the wonderful providence of God. Indeed, we would be doubly ungrateful if, of our own accord, we were to interpose a veil that would obscure the sight of God's favor toward the Church when God himself places his clear mirror before our very eyes.

188

Now one can imagine scarcely anything more scandalous and degrading for the Church in the eyes of the world than the

32. Isa. 7:1-9, *sic, insultus* [cf. vv. 5f.], but perhaps a confusion with Isa. 37:4. [tr.]

exile in Babylon. The cruel plunder of all the [people's] possessions, the countryside horribly ravaged and devastated, their
city destroyed and mutilated by fires and the violence of the
enemy, their temple demolished in dreadful ruins, all its sacred
furnishings shamefully looted — could not all these things have
given them ample justification for reviling their enemies? But
those details I have just mentioned show how insolently and
haughtily the Chaldeans bore themselves. It is indeed very
likely that everywhere they all launched attacks on the worship
of God with insults and with sneers on their faces. But those
things were only so many preliminaries, as it were. After the
people had been carried away to Babylon they were buried like
a dead body in a tomb. Yet there is also this difference: they
were torn in pieces and the parts scattered in all directions to
prevent their coming together again. There was no longer a
royal city of God, no holy place, no sign of worship, no solemn
assemblies; in short, the name of "Church" did not survive.
And to provide the crowning insult, the sacred vessels were put
on show at magnificent and degraded revels (Dan. 5:1-4). Indeed, cruelty reached such a pitch that it was a capital offense to
call upon God (Dan. 3:5f.).

But such a monstrous mass of all sorts of disasters has the
effect of making the power of God more conspicuous in restoring and delivering the people. There is, first of all, the fact that
Daniel and his friends were raised from slavery to positions of
extraordinary influence, so that they brought some alleviation
to the misery of their oppressed brethren (Dan. 2:48f.). This
plainly happened so that it could be a lesson now — that
whenever the Church seems to be utterly abandoned it is still
the object of God's care. That the three holy men who had been
cast into the furnace came out of it safe and sound gave a
particularly clear sign that the liberation of the people would
soon take place (Dan. 3). But the actual return of the people was
deserving of as much wonder as some strange resurrection, so
that the faithful rightly assert in Psalm 126 that they were then
189 like men who dream (v. 1). Then, because provisions were
supplied by the king (Ezra 1), the temple was built at the royal
expense (Ezra 6:8-10), the Jews were protected from violations
by severe decrees (Ezra 6:11f.) — let us think shame of ourselves

if we do not acknowledge that God is the author of those things, when they have been portents to just as many unbelievers. But this reflection cannot express just how great is the value for helping and increasing our faith. Accordingly, people clearly demonstrate their ingratitude when, in a theater so well appointed for the glory of God, they devise for themselves a scandal on which they may stumble.

Moreover, after their return to their own land they received a sudden augmentation in an incredible way, not only in the form of a band of men but also in wealth (Neh. 7:66ff.). This also was no obscure miracle of God's power, especially when enemies were giving them no respite. For we know that they were besieged by as many hostile armies as there were neighboring nations round about them. Indeed, so that God's extraordinary protection might shine out all the more clearly in suffering (*in cruce*), not long afterward they were so overwhelmed by repeated blows of one kind and another that final extermination was at hand. Even if their conditions under the Persian Empire had been tolerable, yet, like sheep destined for slaughter, they were sometimes close to being butchered (Ezra 4).[33] Alexander was restrained by a heavenly oracle from letting loose his enormous forces upon them.[34] In fact, after his death, when the kings of Syria and Egypt were tearing each other to pieces as if they were wild beasts goaded to madness, and neither side was willing to end the raging violence (I Macc. 1:16-19), who would have hoped that the nation lying in between them, and exposed to the passion of both, would survive for long? And there is no doubt that when it was laid low by so many and such different disasters, it would not have remained standing if God had not been its protector and supported it with his hand. At last, under the detestable tyranny of Antiochus, as if plunged into a deep whirlpool, it no longer possessed a glimmer of light in the whole world. The entire countryside was overflowing with innocent blood. Jerusalem was like a pavement covered with a horrible heap of corpses. An accursed idol was set up in the temple. The ordinances of God

---

33. Lit. "the meat market."
34. Josephus, *Antiquities*, XI, ch. 8, ed. Niese (Berlin, 1887-95), vol. III, pp. 62-70. [*B-N*]

having been abolished, the profane and degenerate rites of the heathen held sway instead. All the sacred books were consigned to the flames so that the truth of God might vanish completely from men's memory. Anyone daring to open his mouth, indeed anyone groaning with anguish rather than pollute himself by a treacherous act of hypocrisy, was immediately dragged away to be butchered (I Macc. 1:20-64). The Maccabees gathered a band of people around them; destitute wanderers, they went into hiding among the wild beasts in the caves of the mountains (I Macc. 2:28ff.). In view of the fact that remnants of believers still persisted in such a hopeless situation, and afterwards came out into the open, can anyone deny that they were preserved by the wonderful providence of God? Who would ascribe it to human protection that the books of Moses and the prophets escaped undamaged from those flames?

190

In a word, the history of those times gives us far clearer evidence of the providence of God in protecting and saving the Church than if it had dealt with magnificent and glorious triumphs concerning all the nations. Similarly, other disturbances in which they were afterwards involved hold out a mirror to us. For when the Jews were harassed and ravaged [35] right up to the coming of Christ, as if caught in a never-ending cycle, now by external wars, now by internal factions, and yet again by barbarous and wanton rulers — nevertheless, by the extraordinary providence of God, the fact remains that in the midst of those tempestuous unheavals the Church firmly stood its ground.

Now let us remember so many holy men, yes, and women too, who had to swallow the indignity of those calamities which I have recounted. Some of those people were of advanced years; yet they were forced by necessity to wander through long and involved labyrinths of misfortunes, and at last to die in despair, because they saw no way of escape. There is no doubt that those things were scandals that could have driven them off the right course, and yet, having overcome by faith, they steadily pursued their calling. Now, surely undaunted vivacity such as theirs ought to be not only like a carriage for us, providing relief

---

35. Cf. Josephus, *Antiquities*, XIII-XVIII, ed. Niese, vol. III, 149-IV, 209. [B-N]

for our weariness, but also like wings with which we may fly over lofty rocks, thorny and entangled woods, and any precipitous places whatever. But if the more favorable events which bear witness to God's faithfulness and care in saving the Church do not remove all notions of a scandal from us, we are more delicate and fastidious than it is right to be. What is more, aversion of this sort is not to be tolerated if, when the going is easy, our corrupt imagination makes us put a scandal in our own way.

The Christian Church

Now, if among the people of old the misfortunes and tribulations of the Church always had this blessing — that they brought the more effective help of God with them, and so the more heavily the cross pressed upon them the more clearly God showed that the Church is lifted up and kept on its feet by his hand — under the rule of Christ this reality is seen far more plainly. If for successive periods of peace the Church had maintained a prosperous and attractive state, out of which the gospel had begun to be published to the world, there is no doubt that this would have been the common human condition that everybody would have passed over with contempt. Certainly when the animosities of all nations and classes had from the very start seethed against the little contemptible band; when the name "Christian" was for long an object of such hatred and detestation that on some particular occasions it was nearly obliterated altogether; when everywhere horrible forms of cruelty broke out against all those who were bold enough to give even some covert sign of Christianity; when the whole world was in a conspiracy to destroy the memory of them — the fact that the Church nevertheless somehow survived shows that it had an unusual strength and a secret vigor that defies definition. I mean this, when the Christians had as their temples the hiding-places of wild beasts in the forests and mountains[36] and no safe dwelling anywhere, when they suffered infamy and hatred equally in the extreme, who would not have

191

36. B-N gives references in Tertullian, *Apology*, ch. 2; Eusebius, *History*, III, 33.

been terrified to give his allegiance to the gospel if he had not been moved to do so by God? But the fact is that again and again many people were deliberately and eagerly hastening to submit to such infamy, to that wretchedness and servile fear. As soon as anyone had made open profession of Christ, he was not only hurried away to be put to death but at once was subjected to cruel tortures. There was no pity for sex, none for age. Is it not passing wonderful that any were to be found who were willing to be Christians at this price? As soon as a man was arrested, a most rigorous interrogation was held about his companions. If ever someone who had plotted along with others for the death of a tyrant has kept his tongue under torture so as not to betray his accomplices, everyone marvels at his steadfastness. Do not countless examples, in so many provinces and cities, of faithfulness kept to the end bear witness to the fact that their tongues were under divine control? But when the safety of the entire Church was being jeopardized in individual men, and often in mere women as well, it was certainly an extraordinary and miraculous thing that they were not all utterly destroyed in a short period of time.

But in the midst of so many losses, which were not far short of ruinous, yet the Church never ceased to expand more widely. And that really meant that it was triumphing under the ignominy of the cross. Moreover, anyone who will reflect upon all the circumstances with proper impartiality will acknowledge that among countless deaths there was a continuous sequence of many resurrections. That would be incredible to us because of its difficulty, if someone were to tell us that it will happen in the future; now, when it has taken place, it is not a question of being discerning, but malicious fastidiousness, not only to treat it with contempt but also to consider it as an occasion for a stumbling block.

In Calvin's Day

Certainly the most violent attacks were made in those days, but other ages were also by no means free from the same warfare of the cross. Of course, those who were willing to serve God sincerely and faithfully at that time experienced harder battles. The Roman Empire had surrendered to the rule of Christ. It might seem that the Church was now established on a blessed foundation of quiet and glory. Even barbarian nations had yielded to the possession of Christ. But in the meantime heretical and perfidious men were getting such a grip on things that honest and true ministers were driven from their churches by force and with ignominy too, and were living in exile in distant lands.[37] And even exile would have been denied them if they had not been concealed from their tyrannous enemies. The fact that the Church has often been exposed to such severe and violent persecutions, and that it has lain almost prostrate under the feet of its enemies, is quite inconsistent with a spectacle of worldly dignity. But the fact that a smaller number of the godly, with an unconquerable firmness of faith, surmounted such great waves of persecution, and the fact that the Church survived all tyrants and heretics in order to pass on the true doctrine of the faith to succeeding generations, provides a shining testimony of the divine power, because it far surpasses all the glories of the world. In the Church's present adversity no dignity like that shines out to bring the heavenly kingdom of God before the eyes of men. For when it has been overwhelmed, its enemies, with the title of the chief one himself,[38] and equipped as if with booty, crush it under foot with both cruelty and pride. If anyone has ventured to offer even the slightest resistance to their ungodliness, they are formidable with sword, fire, and tortures of every kind, and leave hardly a place for the true Church in the whole earth.

192

But if it does find a few corners for itself, and it is now attacked with force of arms, now harassed by scoffers, and now tormented by threats and terrors, it is displaying nothing less than that royal dignity (*decorem*) of Christ that is so greatly commended by the prophets. Certainly when the ungodly, with their threats and terrorizing and their furious raging, however, do not go so far that the Church of God does not stay

---

37. *B-N* gives references to Eusebius, *Vita Constantini*, IV; Athanasius, *Apologia contra Arianos*, 3-19.
38. *B-N* puts this reference after "enemies": "He is thinking of the Pope (according to the French version)." [*B-N*] And so of the papists. This is the most satisfactory way to translate the misleading and ambiguous *summi hostes ipsius titulo*. [tr.]

firm and erect under the humiliation of the cross, why then do we not give great praise to the glory of God for preserving it so marvelously? If anyone with experience of the events turns over in his own mind just how many things the ungodly have contrived for its destruction during these thirty years, he will be forced to marvel that it was not completely wiped out a hundred times. And now, although it breaks the hearts of many people that in less than two years it has been miserably torn in pieces, and its mangled parts are not very far from the lion's jaws, in the end the faithful will perceive that this took place according to God's very good purpose, so that the stretching out of his hand to deliver it might be all the more obvious. For we acknowledge that it is saved by him only when it has been snatched away from death.

Finally, yet another reason is to be added to this, that it is absolutely essential that our unruly spirit be tamed and subjugated by the discipline of the cross. We see that while the Church flourished with spiritual vigor in the midst of troubles, it has melted away when it has enjoyed peace too much. Today, when the Lord holds us in check with a tight and strict bridle, we see that everywhere nearly all are leading wanton lives. What would happen if they were given the chance to run riot without restriction? When the profession of the gospel held sway far and wide in Germany, and the forces were still complete of those who seemed disposed to support the good cause, and when, confident in this, they undertook that lamentable war, everything turned out unfavorably.[39] While people's spirits were raised to high hopes for our side, I said publicly on some occasions[40] that more danger threatens us from our own victory than from that of our enemies, and that no disasters are to be feared so much as what I may call a highly triumphal gospel, which would transport us to a state of elation. And indeed today I still do not regret that statement. If the Lord had not been quick to resist their ungodly presumption, the disease would have become almost incurable in the course of time. Teaching and godly admonitions would have carried no

193

39. The Schmalkaldic War, 1546-1547. [B-N]
40. "In sermons (according to the French version); but no reference is to be found there." [B-N]

weight. Like unbroken animals, those who could not yet bear to receive tolerable discipline would have burst the whole yoke with violent force. So great was the stain of this infamy that it could have been removed from the gospel only if those who had previously not been disposed to learn moderation of their own accord had been compelled to do so by force and misfortunes.

Again, by this testing the Lord revealed what sort of character each one had. Haughtily they were all casting the gospel under a shadow. In many places the leading positions were filled by wicked hypocrites. In fact, after suffering defeat, certain leaders of great reputation, the nobles of a state paralyzed by an indefinable fear, were immediately demoralized and freely surrendered. In this they openly displayed more than effeminate softness — I should rather say treacherous cowardice. In one nation we see more impious and sacrilegious defections from Christ in the space of two years than the histories of all times and peoples narrate. Indeed, in others it has been made plain how faith remains firm and unbroken when hearts are sustained by the power of the Spirit. The heroic magnanimity of soul which the Lord made plain for all generations to see in one man, who was defeated and a captive, would never have been believed except from such an experience of the cross.[41] I am deliberately passing over some remarkable examples of that kind, which it would be easy to cite. But let each one ponder these, and countless others, in his own mind. They say now that women are being dragged off to death[42] because not only their husbands but also the whole populace are lacking in mercy; for, in order to gain the brief enjoyment of fleeting peace in this world, those people had no hesitation in denying that the Son of God is the author of eternal life and in freeing themselves from his heavenly rule.

Finally, the Lord himself knows better what future benefit lies in the things that are now commonly regarded as serious misfortunes. For our part we must bravely accept whatever calamities may befall, hoping that the Lord will give a conclu-

41. "He is referring to John Frederick, Duke of Saxony, a prisoner from 1547-1552." [B-N, q.v. for bibliography]
42. "In many provinces of Germany (according to the French version)." [B-N]

sion such as we should desire. Indeed, we ought always to hold this principle in our minds, that whenever the Church is temporarily oppressed, the very good Father, who exercises an extraordinary care of his own, will never allow it to be overwhelmed and disappear. If Christ must "rule in the midst of his enemies" (Ps. 110:2), as was shown long ago by the witness of the Spirit, then his Kingdom cannot be in our midst without warfare and continuous fighting. If we are like sheep destined for slaughter, but, on the other hand, our adversaries are inflamed with madness like wolves, let us remember that precept of the Lord's, that "we must possess our souls in patience" (Luke 21:19), until he himself "perfects his power in our weakness" (II Cor. 12:9). Surely the apostles were never more blessed than when they fearlessly cried out, "Why are the Gentiles in an uproar, and why do the peoples imagine vain things?" (Acts 4:25).[43] If we grasp the meaning of the words "God in heaven laughs" (Ps. 2:4), when he gives free rein to the ungodly [Ps. 2:3], we too shall scoff fearlessly at the whole world, even if it is in arms, for we have been provided with the same confidence as the apostles.

Original Sin

Next there come scandals which, once again, are commonly believed to spring from doctrine, but which in fact are the characteristic and genuine products of either human forwardness, ignorance, or curiosity. The teaching of Scripture about the corruption of our nature is that, because we bear an innate corruption and badness from the womb, it is accordingly impossible to produce anything from a bad tree but bad fruit, until we are restored to wholeness by the grace of Christ. In this connection human reason concludes not only that men themselves are free from blame when they sin, but that the blame can justifiably be ascribed to God, who creates them such that they seem to be born to sin. Let each one examine his own conscience and he will be convicted and silenced at once. For there we shall discover what Scripture bears witness to so often, that the

---

43. *Tumultuantur.* Cf. *Vulg., fremuerunt.* [tr.]

source of all our faults is the perverseness that clings to us. We are eager to perpetrate all sorts of evils precisely because that is displeasing to God.

Why does it happen, then, that whenever some guilty men are disturbed within by their own consciences they eagerly search everywhere for empty excuses to free themselves and others from guilt, and, not content with that, also call God to account? If they were not freely disposed to deceive themselves into their own destruction, would they not be condemning the fault that they discover in themselves rather than transferring the cause of it elsewhere? But, come now, since they are merely seeking any sort of excuse for their blasphemies, let us point out in a single word that they are reviling, shamelessly and without excuse. When it is evident that a man sins of his own free will, will he boast of his innocence? When they have had their full say, they must come in the end to this: God charges them only with what they commit of their own accord. And what human being will absolve them when they do wrong voluntarily? Moreover, will God not be allowed to condemn what men justly condemn? But yet they find fault with God because he has not given them a better mind, and also a more upright heart, as if he had not in fact given those things in the beginning. For our teaching does not hold the perverseness, which rules in us, agreeable to the creation of God, but ascribes it to our corrupt nature.

Again, they take exception that it is unjust for the punishment of another's wrongdoing to be inflicted on themselves. There would perhaps be some excuse for that exception if they themselves were free from personal sin and showed that they are burdened by another's guilt. But since they have lost their righteous nature in their first parent in such a way that they are vicious of their own free will, why do they complain that injustice is being done to them, as if they were innocent? Of course, they are doing what the most desperate robbers usually do; while they are being hurried away for punishment, they rail at the judge with insults picked up from all sorts of places. Again and again there are men like that — just as ready to commit crimes as they are fluent in the use of abusive language. But what do they accomplish with such fierce insults? Their

195

own disgrace is not lessened, nor is the judge branded with any stigma. And they are aware of that themselves, but in their blind desperation they derive a poor comfort from their ridiculous revenge.

Up to now I have been replying to the blasphemies of those who show their ungodliness openly. But the calumnies of Sadoleto, Pighi, and others like them remain, and by these they are bringing our teaching into disrepute, as if it were dragging along with it a variety of almost countless absurdities.[44] Indeed, if anything out of it is regarded as a scandal, it is because our writings are not being read. What am I to do, therefore, but exhort all those who are carried away by an unreasonable aversion and are avoiding the unknown truth not to bring on themselves the twofold penalty of their rashness? For in the first place, they are defrauding themselves of the salvation offered to them, and, in the second place, they will not escape punishment because, without hearing the case for the defense, they immediately pronounce it a second lie.[45]

Predestination

What else can account for the fact that predestination is a veritable sea of scandals except our curiosity of forwardness? Here the point at issue is the secret judgment of God, whose glory is such that if men come too near, their minds must be not only stunned and stupefied but completely consumed by it. And yet the Lord has revealed in Scripture as much as our power of comprehension allows and as much as matters to us, that we are all undoubtedly lost, except those he redeems from death by electing them to life, that the grace of Christ reaches only to those who had been preordained to salvation by free election before they were born, and that others remain in their sins as they have been destined for eternal destruction. But to probe beyond that, even if it were permissible, would not be to our advantage. Now, since it is just as impious as it is harmful for us to force our way through, the Lord holds us back from

44. For a reference to a letter of Sadoleto, see *B-N* footnote.
45. Original Sin is the first lie. Both Sadoleto and Pighi wrote on Original Sin. See also p. 11. [tr.]

doing so as if he laid his hand on us, and on our part it is our duty to embrace reverently what the Lord teaches, and, being content with that, to refrain from all other questioning. For the true rule of wisdom in this connection is to be so self-controlled as to desire to know no more than what is revealed in Scripture. Certainly God has had no intention of hiding anything from us, except what was superfluous for us to know or too abstruse for our powers of comprehension. We are all the more ungrateful if we do not temper our eagerness for asking questions to that method which he himself has maintained in teaching.

Why, therefore, are we to wonder if those who, like madmen, rush with violent force against God, hurl themselves into an abyss, or dash themselves on rocks? They accuse God of 196 being a tyrant because he condemns men to destruction before they were born. But one day they will realize that he is a just judge. I should rather say that they already feel that in their own hearts, even if they may not acknowledge it. They plead that it is useless to give moral precepts, that it is pointless to make laws, and that it is even unjust to carry out sentences for the punishment of criminals when all things are governed or rather rotated by fate. As if God does not in fact guide his elect by the Holy Spirit and allow Satan to torment the reprobate, so as to give to the former the teaching of piety and profitable exhortations, and to hold the latter convicted of contumacy — and that without excuse because, having been warned, they did not submit.

I pass over how they gain nothing by artfully discrediting the providence of God by giving it the name of fate. For we do not talk foolishly about an intricacy of connected causes with the Stoics, or subject the government of the world to the stars, or invent a necessity in the very nature of things; but that, of course, is what profane men call "fate." The predestination of God is, therefore, quite a different thing from fate. But let us be done with a battle over words. "If," they say, "the necessity of things is fixed by the eternal decree of God, it is useless to teach what the nature of everybody's duty is. For teaching will not alter in the slightest what has been determined already."[46] Yet

---

46. See *Inst.*, III, xxiii, 12ff. [B-N]

they ought to ponder once again that teaching has also been ordained by God himself for the purpose of serving his secret purposes. Will not teaching, like an outstretched hand, lead those whom he has preordained to life by his eternal adoption to the place which he has appointed? For what else is effectual calling but the fulfillment of the election that was previously hidden? He takes the reprobate to task with various rebukes, and, it seems, without any success. But since he renders them inexcusable in this way, teaching appears to have some force in their case also. Foolish men do not perceive how the works of God harmonize with each other in a beautiful order. As a result, they rashly set up a conflict between teaching, which is nothing else but the handmaid of his eternal will, and that will itself.

Let us learn accordingly that God does not speak to men in order to remove, or even correct, the things that he once decreed by himself, but rather in order to prove by the actual effect how fixed and unchanging they are. It is impossible that those whom he elected once for all from the beginning should perish; but because he does not intend them to perish, he hands them over to the faithful guardianship of Christ. Furthermore, in order to have Christ, the Shepherd by whom they are protected, it is necessary for them to be gathered into his fold. Therefore, since the elect obtain salvation by hearing the voice of the Shepherd, their election is brought to its realization only by the external preaching of the gospel. He also orders the same preaching to be set before the reprobate. Why? In order that he may overturn what he has determined about their destruction? No! On the contrary, it is in order that their obstinate disbelief might make all the plainer how the grace of secret election prevails. For can one imagine any brighter mirror in which this grace may shine out clearly than this: when in a situation of common teaching the same call of God, the identical instrument of calling, there is so great a distinction between men that some firmly reject what others obediently embrace? However, at the same time we see that even if the word which a man utters may not change the hearts of unbelievers, it may nevertheless prick their consciences and, like a bridle, put a check on their wantonness.

197

PART II: THE SECOND CLASS
OF SCANDALS: TROUBLES
OF VARIOUS KINDS

The Gospel Brings Strife

And now we must turn to the discussion of the scandals which we assigned to the second category.[1] Many complain that the gospel is the source of dissensions because as soon as it comes on the scene controversies spring up along with it, and worse, just as if the trumpet had sounded the call to battle, men take up arms against each other. We must indeed acknowledge the truth of Christ's statement that along with the gospel dissensions and fights invariably arise (Matt. 10:34). But we must consider when exactly that may happen.

In the first place, as I have already said, it may happen if men in their obstinacy rebel when God wishes to bring them to order. It is difficult for men who are supremely confident in their own wisdom to allow themselves to be taught by Christ. Now when passions of the flesh rule in men like so many wild and untamed beasts, need we wonder if they offer violent resistance to a yoke and bridle? But it is quite intolerable that the gospel should be given the blame for an evil which is to be found in ourselves.

Those who shrink from the doctrine of peace because of their fear of troubles and hatred of dissensions are quite in the wrong. They think there is nothing better than peaceful conditions. Suppose therefore that some tyrant, in his enormity and cruelty, arises as a result of this attitude; when he seizes noble

1. See pp. 13-14 above.

virgins and matrons for his own purposes, strips all the rich of their possessions, murders and massacres the innocent, so that all are paralyzed and struck dumb with fear, will tyranny deserve praise on this pretext? Now, if we ask what exactly is that peace which many are sure they would gain by rejecting the gospel, it will indeed be clear that corrupt and perverted religions prevail in undisturbed peace, because Satan, the worst tyrant of them all, exults with impunity over half-dead men. All the same, as far as outward subjection of the body is concerned, perhaps it may sometimes be better to put up with that rather than, for the sake of asserting our freedom, start a disturbance that may break out into slaughter and disorder on a vast scale. But when it is a question of the eternal destruction of the soul, nothing ought to be so prized that it causes us to long for, or even cultivate of our own free will, a peace that brings death with it.

Also, what is to be said about our defrauding the Son of God of his rightful sovereignty in this way? But it would be better for heaven to be confounded with earth rather than that the honor given him by the Father be diminished, not to mention its being taken away and abrogated altogether. Shall we clearly live alienated from the Prince of Life? Shall we make open war against God in order to be at peace with men? So that we may not be forced into a quarrel with the ungodly, shall we not refuse to be separated from Christ, through whom we are reconciled to God along with the angels? Indeed, that reward is more than we deserve. And in fact when Christ describes the kingdom of Satan as one at peace, he is not teaching that it is to be desired greatly for that very reason; on the contrary, he is promising that this will prove to be of the greatest advantage so that the stronger one fighting with Satan may strip him of his unjust tyranny (Luke 11:21f.). For if we see people who fight eagerly for power [pro imperio] or for their own freedom being bold and unhesitating in facing all sorts of uprisings, when Satan causes violent disturbances to throw the Kingdom of Christ into confusion, ought we not to be offering resistance with a far braver spirit? Son will rise up against father; father will not spare the life of son; brother will lie in wait for brother (Matt. 10:21, 35). Is the purpose of these prophecies to make

198

men guarded in their attitude to the gospel? Rather, is it not that, having been warned in time, they may not be filled with terror by the strangeness it brings? For I am only concerned with those who take advantage of the name of Christ to make it the pretext for a spurious peace. Yet I am also aware that in causing dissensions the troublemakers are the tools of Satan, serving his purpose of inflaming otherwise quiet men with a hatred of the gospel. So in our generation, just after the gospel has begun to be revived, he has stirred up cruel men to declare open war on laws, courts of justice, and the whole political order [*omni politiae*]. But since we are by no means unacquainted with trickery of that sort, if we only seek peace from the heart, we shall genuinely experience that God is offering it to us through the gospel, and as a result we may stand fast among men. To stand apart from the gospel because it may stir up dissensions is certainly quite wrong.

Ungodly Living

This looks like a more reasonable ground for a scandal. As soon as the gospel begins to be proclaimed, many people who previously had appeared to be religious erupt into ungodliness as if a spring has been opened. But it would be nearer the truth to say that this is valuable for confirming faith. When Simeon assigns to Christ this function of "revealing the thoughts of many hearts" (Luke 2:35), his statement as such is acceptable in so far as nobody opposes it. Therefore, when it actually does take place, why should it be considered absurd? Let us suppose[2] that it was never said, so that we may bring an unprejudiced judgment to bear on what we see before our eyes.

Whereas thirty years ago[3] religion was flourishing everywhere, and all were in agreement about the common and customary worship of God, without any controversy, now ungodliness and contempt for God are breaking out on all sides. In the first place I say that if light is scattering the darkness, there is nothing extraordinary about it. Even long ago it was a generally accepted proverb that the hidden recesses of the human

2. Reading *fingamus* for *fingagmus*. [tr.]
3. That is, 1520 in the unreformed Church. [tr.]

heart are so deep, and its secret places so tortuous, that there is
scarcely an abyss in existence to be compared with them. Now,
if there is anything in which men are deceitful and hypocritical
it is in the astonishingly impudent way they make a mockery of
199   God at the slightest justification. Add to that Satan's cunning
trick in displaying the extraordinary showiness of a religion,
which is no religion at all, partly by drawing over a cloud of
ignorance, partly by masking and hiding the worship of God
with ceremonies. All with eyes to see are aware that this was the
case under the Papacy. For in it consciences are benumbed as
though cast under the spell of venomous charms, and they
escape by means of long and labyrinthine ways from a serious
awareness of God. For that vast chaos of ceremonies is indeed
"a den of robbers" (Jer. 7:11; Matt. 21:13) because hypocrites,
hiding behind their cover, are confident that they are at liberty
to do anything they like with impunity. If unconcern like that
takes away the distinction between true and false religion, then
there is nothing extraordinary about it. Even if they ever do
appear to be getting nearer to God, the only object of their
wearying themselves so much and of tormenting themselves to
such an extent is that the wickedness of their hearts, soothed by
such remedies, may remain quiet within them. Now if, after
the torch of the gospel has been brought in, hypocrisy is routed
and ungodliness is made plain to see, it is unjust and wrong to
take any offense at that.

Long ago among unredeemed men the only people to be
regarded as despisers of the gods were the public sorcerer, the
will-forger [*testamentarius*], the perjurer, and the man who was
a thorough scoundrel. For when carnal men were inventing
gods for themselves, it was the easiest thing in the world to
have nothing more to do with religion. But yet we are aware
that the prophets inveigh vehemently against scoffers, and
there is no doubt that they have grave reasons for doing so.
Therefore, when ungodliness was making itself felt in the
Church of God, unbelievers at that time looked upon it as
something trivial. Or shall we say for that reason that the law
and the prophets served to fan it into flames? Or will that be a
reason for discounting the pure religion, which was dragging
forth that many-headed monster into the light of day? No! for

even in the very Church of God it was only after the birth of Isaac that Ishmael appeared as a mocker (Gen. 21:9).[4] He who at an earlier stage was next to holy Abraham suddenly broke out into vicious derision of the grace of God, so that he deserved to be cast out from his father's family. Or should such an example as Abraham have cast off members of his household from the sacred family? Moreover, what was vaguely shadowed forth in Isaac ought to have been expressed more clearly in Christ, and the gospel story does in fact bear witness to that. For since he himself has come into the world, we know how great an eruption of madness has come from those who previously used to vaunt themselves as "religious." Therefore, let us hear no more of the wicked opinion that, because unrestrained ungodliness is dragged forth into the light of day as if from hiding places, it springs from the teaching of the gospel. On the contrary, let the very fact that "the thoughts of many hearts are laid bare" be something that gives us pleasure.

Rejecters of the Gospel and God's Reaction

However, another reason for this situation must also be observed. While some reject the proffered grace of the gospel, others take only a contemptuous nibble at it, and still others proudly repudiate it, does not all their ingratitude deserve that God exact no ordinary vengeance on it? And he does indeed punish them severely when he throws them into that fearful state of blindness which deprives them of their religious perception. Therefore, let us realize that all the sceptics,[5] whom today we see mocking at the whole religion of Christ, and all the Epicureans, whom we see exposing themselves — with no fear of God — to any profligacy they like, are just so many examples of the vengeance of God, which he has placed before our eyes to commend the dignity and value of the gospel to us. Paul is quite right in saying that those who had wrongfully suppressed such knowledge of God as can be obtained from looking at the

200

4. "Mocking" is a wrong translation for "playing." See *RV* mgn., *RSV*, *Vulg.*, and commentaries. [tr.]
5. *Lucianicos homines*. Presumably from Lucian of Samosata, cynic, poet, satirist, sceptic of the second century A.D. See *ODCC*, 841a.

universe alone, were given up to "a reprobate mind" and to the vile and full passions of lewdness, so that those who had defrauded God of his honor received the just reward for their ingratitude when they were subjected to the utmost ignominy (Rom. 1:28). Since contempt of the gospel is a more intolerable sacrilege, it is no wonder if more severe vengeance is now exacted on it. But why should that be? Well, while agreeing that those who allowed the tiny sparks appearing in the workshop of the universe to be put out by their own folly were justly punished, would we wish those who with deliberate malice eclipse and extinguish the full splendor of the glory of God, which shines in the gospel, to scoff at God with impunity? Now, if God is more than justified in severely punishing contempt or rejection of his grace, why do we take offense at seeing examples of his vengeance, when it is to be given the highest praise? On the contrary, as I have already said, just as God affirms the majesty of the gospel in this way, so it was fitting that reverence for him be established in our minds.

How can the gospel by which he offers and gives himself to us in the person of his Son be received in a way that is worthy enough? Yet there are many who think this incomparable treasure hardly deserving of common respect; others throw it down at their feet; others carelessly neglect it for the empty pleasures of the world; and there are even many who jestingly turn it into a common entertainment, as if it were some sort of show. What is the upshot? Although at least some religion might have dwelt in their souls, they are now barking at God like dogs. Indeed they pride themselves on their sharpness of mind, and in addition they seem to be demigods because they have no hesitation about offering insults to heaven. But if the changing of a man into a beast is an unnatural thing, we should really deplore them all the more because they are not touched by any sorrow for their wrongdoing. They make witty mockery of the absurdities of the papists, but they themselves deserve never to go back to the papacy. For it is not fitting that there should be normal deaths for those to whom the sacred blood of Christ, the eternal truth of God, and the light of life have come to be things provoking not merely laughter but also derision. And without a doubt the contempt of the gospel that now prevails everywhere definitely indicates some kind of brutish life. For since the Lord, shining on men with his gospel, is the ultimate remedy for curing their lives, it is evident that those for whom this medicine does no good are incurable. Indeed, those who knowingly and willingly either avoid the medicine or keep it at a distance are responsible for bringing death, in all sorts of guises, on themselves. I conclude this paragraph by saying that those who regard ungodliness as the horrible evil it in fact is conclude from the severity of this punishment how seriously the Lord regards contempt of his gospel. Furthermore, this serves as a warning to strengthen them in their faith in him and their obedience to him. It is common knowledge that Agrippa, Villanovanus, Dolet[6] and their like have always proudly rejected the gospel, as if they were so many Cyclops. They have finally lapsed so far into folly and madness that not only did they spread execrable blasphemies against the Son of God,[7] but also, in regard to the question of the life of the soul, they held that they themselves were no different from dogs and pigs.[8] Others, like Rabelais, Deperius and Goveanus,[9] having sampled the gospel, have been struck with the same blindness.[10] And what is the reason for that except that they had previously profaned that sacred pledge of eternal life by making a mockery and a laughingstock of it,[11] with the impudence of the impious. Let us realize that the Lord is pointing out, as if with his finger, all those with natures like theirs as a warning to

6. Heinrich Cornelius Agrippa von Nettesheim (1486-1535), "Christian Skeptic," particularly in *De Incertitudine;* see *ODCC,* pp. 26 f. Michael Servetus, born Miguel Servede (or Serveto) at Tudela, 1511; he was brought up at Villanova, near Lérida, in northeastern Spain, thus accounting for the use of the name Villanovanus; see *ODCC,* p. 1263. Etienne Dolet (1509-1546), French "martyr of the Renaissance"; see *E.Brit. Mic.,* III, 604b,c. [tr.] For other Calvin references, the works of these men, and other references to them, see *B-N,* nn. 1, 2. [tr.]
7. Capnius to Calvin, 1542, *CR,* XI, 490 ff. [*B-N*]
8. For references to Dolet, Rabelais, and a possible source for the reference to "dogs and pigs" in Agrippa's *De Incertitudine,* see *B-N,* n. 3. [tr.]
9. Deperius is Jean Bonaventure Des Périers (1500-1544), storyteller, humanist, freethinker, author of the satirical *Cymbalum Mundi* (1537), a bitter and violent attack on Christianity; see *E.Brit. Mic.,* III, 491b. Goveanus is presumably André Gouvéa, principal of the Collège de Guyenne at Bordeaux, where Montaigne and George Buchanan were his pupils; see *NCMH,* II, 423, 437. In *E.Brit.* (9th ed., 1876), IV, 412b, he is referred to as Andrew Govea. [tr.]
10. *B-N* gives references to *Pantagruel* by Rabelais.
11. Rabelais, *Gargantua and Pantagruel;* Des Périers, *Cymbalum Mundi.* [*B-N*]

us, so that we may anxiously press on in the race[12] to which we are called, so that nothing similar may befall us.

The Spread of Atheistic Views

Furthermore, not only do those corrupt men upset the weak by their own fall or downfall, but they pour out the poison of their ungodliness in all directions, so that they fill the world with atheism. This scandal must also be opposed. And the Spirit is doing that when he warns that "mockers shall come to attack our hope with mockery" (II Pet. 3:3f.). But he also says that fickle souls will be susceptible to their charms (II Pet. 2:2). Therefore, in order that we may be beyond danger we must acquire steadfastness in Christ. It is the usual custom of those filthy dogs to play the role of the buffoon in order that they may have greater license for belching out blasphemies. Thus, at feasts and in discussions, in their pleasant, jocular way, they overthrow all the principles of religion.[13] But first of all, indeed, they ingratiate themselves with slanted witticisms. However, what they are after is to obliterate all fear of God from the minds of men.[14] For they finally break through to the point that all religions have their origins in men's brains, that God exists because it pleases men to believe so,[15] that the hope of eternal life has been invented to deceive the simple, and that the fear of judgment is childish terror.[16]

These Siren voices are certainly too inclined to soothe the ears of many people; but the same ears are already being tickled by their own itching. For we see some people who strive and chase so eagerly after things which make for the destruction of a sense of piety that before they have scarcely had time to hear a few words they beat a hasty retreat from the eternal and un-changeable truth of God. And, of course, anyone who has been even moderately versed in the sacred Scriptures and who has proved that our faith has been founded on something far removed

12. *Stadio.* "1550 has, wrongly, *studio.*" [B-N]
13. As n. 7, p. 61.
14. Gouvéa, *Epigrammata.* [B-N]
15. Rabelais, *Pantagruel, Prognostion,* ch. 1. [B-N]
16. Rabelais, *Pantagruel.* [B-N]

from opinion will not waver in his opinion so easily. Indeed, when they are assailed by those stratagems, there is little chance of yielding in those who have the sign of the Spirit engraved on their hearts. But Paul is saying the same thing, that men "make shipwreck of their faith when they cut loose from a good conscience" (I Tim. 1:19). By this he means not only that "a good conscience" is the preserver of right understanding, but also that it is not to be wondered at if those who are tossed this way and that among the varying storms of their passions are completely lacking in stability. Therefore, there is no cause for atheism to perturb us even if it is rampant everywhere throughout the world, and in fact chiefly holds sway in the courts of kings[17] and princes, in courts of justice, and in other distinguished walks of life.[18] For if I were to ask people with experience of affairs — thus those very ones who cannot extricate themselves from this temptation — how many would concede that a good conscience is given hospitable treatment in those places, the answer will be an easy one, that it is banished altogether. Then why are we surprised at that "shipwreck of faith" which, Paul teaches, follows inevitably?

Moreover, if all who are affected by the love of money keep it   203
hidden so carefully in chests, the man who is not fortified and defended by the fear of God exposes himself on his own responsibility to being plundered. What excuse will he then plead if he is stripped of faith, the heavenly treasure, particularly when we know nothing so deadly as those little snares of the ungodly? For there is to be no weakening in spirit, because danger threatens from those people; indeed, I warn and testify that there are no serpents with venom so poisonous. In fact, for that reason we ought to be more vigilant and alert in keeping guard. However, I say that all who have not neglected to plant firm roots in Christ will be free from this exceedingly pestilential contagion. And, of course, that is not my dictum but Paul's: "We must grow in the knowledge of Christ, until we attain to mature manhood, so

17. Reading *in regum et principum aulis* for *regnum*, with the French "aux cours des rois et des princes." [tr.]
18. The French version of 1550 reads, "In the courts of kings and princes, among men of the law-courts, prothonotaries and other wearers of the round cap; among gentlemen, treasurers, and stout merchants." [B-N]

that we may be no longer subject to the cunning of men who try to circumvent us" (Eph. 4:13f.). Yet at the same time we must give heed to another exhortation of Paul: seeing that we have been betrothed to the Son of God, on condition that we may remain completely faithful to that husband, we must especially beware that Satan does not seduce us with his pandering ways (II Cor. 11:2ff.). For if a woman who has listened to the voice of seductive allurements is considered to have given some sign of unfaithfulness already, it is evident that souls who find it a delight to be incited to treacherous defection are far from chaste.

Errors: Rooted in Personal Faults

All errors have a similar cause. Many waver in their faith, and others even withdraw from the gospel altogether, because they contend that it is a field of error. It is indeed as if a man would have nothing to do with the cultivating and sowing of the ground because pure seed often degenerates into crab grass. So that the strangeness of the situation might not discourage anyone, Christ warned that this would happen (Matt. 13:24ff.). For in that passage, even if he compares hypocrites to tares and the true and genuine sons of God to wheat, he is showing that it is, however, Satan's usual trickery to spoil and corrupt God's heavenly seed in any way he can to prevent its coming to maturity. We know that the world has long lain barren like a desert and an uncultivated field. Now God has planted the doctrine of the gospel at the hands of his ministers. Are we surprised if Satan mixes in every possible corruption? And did he not bring in false doctrines by the wagonload as soon as the gospel began to spring up? There are countless numbers whom I pass over. But can anything stranger be imagined than the ravings of Valentinus, Montanus, and the Manichees? It is indeed extremely amusing that those who think it something of a miracle that the light of the gospel was not extinguished by such thick darkness, and who hear with approbation that it has stood strong and invincible against so many stratagems, are being moved to hostility to the doctrine of the gospel because Satan is now also pouring out the darkness of his lies. Indeed, because people are upset by this difficulty in various ways, I shall show briefly that the only kind of stumbling block there is, is that against which individuals run of their own accord — or because of stupidity or some other fault of their own.

Sects and Heresies

There are those who make simply one allegation, that sects spring forth from the teaching of the gospel. Now some of these lay hold of any pretext whatever, while others too light-heartedly transfer the cause of evil to the gospel, when it actually resides elsewhere. Whoever will deign to open his eyes will see that the gospel is not only the pure and clear truth of God but the supreme bond of sacred unity. Now, if Satan rises up in opposition, he is making it his business to obscure this light with clouds of errors and to tear to pieces the unity into which the sons of God are growing. For he is the father of lies and the author and contriver of all divisions. For that reason it is our responsibility to labor more earnestly in seeking the truth, and when we have found it to embrace it more firmly. Those people not only abstain and flee from every such endeavor but also set this particular defensive shield against God, to avoid being forced to yield obedience to his authority.

Though others have given attention to sound doctrine, they do not look for a way to reject it; yet when they do draw back in a state of agitation at the slightest opportunity, they do not have a reasonable excuse. But if they are uncertain about what way they should move, and show that they are pliant, then they are certainly justified in fearing that they may then be entangled in the chains of errors by this easiness of theirs. Well, that is something; but there is another and better way to guard against this danger: to submit themselves to God in pious humility, modesty, sobriety, and reverence. For Christ was not giving an empty promise when he said that the door will be opened to those who knock (Matt. 7:7). And it is not without good cause that the Spirit of judgment and discernment has been bestowed by the Father.[19] And it was also not for nothing that the Lord

204

---

19. Reading *spiritus* for *spiritu*. [tr.]

promised through the mouth of Isaiah that he himself would be the teacher of his people, and that he would be behind them to direct their steps (Isa. 30:21). Finally, so that we may not be cheated or disappointed, he tells us that the way of life is pointed out to us in his Word. From this it is clear that a good many men intellectually seek after the Word itself, but they end up paralyzed in trouble of their own making because they despise its remedies.

We see many gripped by different errors being led away from the right way; but that is something that never happens except as the just punishment of God. In the first place, Augustine is right in describing pride as the mother of all heresies.[20] For there has never been a teacher of error who has not been brought to his downfall by perverted ambition. We know that God is a faithful teacher of little children; we know that Christ calls to himself as his disciples those who are humble and gentle. Therefore, it is not surprising that those who are swollen with arrogance are driven from this school, to be dragged this way and that by their own inconclusive speculations. In our own time there are many who have fallen away from the pure teaching of the gospel and have begun to be the authors of false dogmas. We shall find that all of them have been attacked by the disease of pride and have created intellectual tortures for themselves and others.

205   Out of many let the one example of Servetus suffice.[21] For this man, who was already puffed up with Portuguese pride, and is now even more swollen with his own arrogance, made up his mind that the best way to make a name for himself was to overthrow all the principles of religion. Accordingly, not only does he repudiate as absurd all that was taught by the Fathers ever since the Apostolic Age itself, and accepted by all believers all down the course of the ages, but he also criticizes it and tears it to pieces with the cruelest of insults.[22] Now, that furious dog-like biting and barking which fills all the pages of

20. See B-N for references.
21. French version, 1550, reads, "There is a certain Spaniard called Servetus, who plays the doctor, calling himself Villeneuve. This poor conceited fellow was already puffed up with the arrogance of Portugal." [B-N] See n. 6, p. 61. [tr.]
22. Inst., I, xiii, 22. [B-N]

his writings is evidence enough of the kind of spirit that drives the man. Indeed, if one looks into the matter he will clearly see that, burning with a desperate thirst for vainglory, he has eagerly swallowed all the craziest and absurdest things and made himself drunk with them. He imagines that the Word [*sermonem*] of God did not exist before Moses introduces God speaking in the creation of the world.[23] When God put forth such great power as he did, it is as if he actually began to exist only then rather than that he gave evidence of his eternal being. Servetus deifies the flesh of Christ in such a way that, the reality of his human nature having been destroyed, he imagines that his divinity, which is spiritual, is palpable.[24] And yet when he boldly[25] calls Christ God, some vague shadowy specter is invented for us, inasmuch as Christ was merely a Platonic "idea" from the beginning; and he is the Son of God only by the right that he was conceived in the womb of the Virgin by the Holy Spirit.[26] At the same time Servetus collects many wagon-loads of speculations which are so meaningless that it is easy for any sensible man to see that only someone bewitched by a blind love of himself can be so foolish. But as soon as the truth of God has come on the scene, if both their ambition rouses and Satan stimulates arrogant inclinations so that they either conceal or overthrow it with perverse fictions and fanatical opinions, that is no reason why we need to be upset as if it were something unusual.

Therefore, just as pride is the mother of all heresies, as I have already said, so the vanity of those who attach themselves as disciples to such teachers is the nurse that perpetually fosters heresies. As often as some error is being spread by a false prophet, Moses tells us that we are being tested as to whether we love the Lord with all our heart (Deut. 13:2-4). What is the point of that except that we may know that the only people who are led away from the pure doctrine are those who make a counterfeit show and a false profession of piety? Those stratagems certainly do not destroy faith that is fixed with firm

206

23. *Ibid.*, I, xiii, 8. [*B-N*]
24. See *Inst.*, II, xiv, 8. [*B-N*]
25. Lit. "with full cheeks" (*plenis buccis*); see also n. 28, p. 71 below.
26. See *Inst.*, II, xiv, 5. *B-N* wrongly has II, iv, 5. [tr.]

roots but rather illustrate its strength; just as Paul writes that when sects are raging in the Church, those "who are genuine are made manifest" (I Cor. 11:19). Thus it is not at all surprising that, when the wind of some new sect has been blowing, very many are scattered in all directions, since very few have the fear of God firmly fixed in their souls. It is far from right for us to waver with the crowd.

Pride and Its Effects

For a long time now it has been customary for many people to use the gospel as a handle for their impudence. It is not without good reason that the apostles so often warn about keeping liberty in check, in case it might be turned into license of the flesh. For if the slightest opportunity presents itself, the flesh always runs riot at once. And since bondage is hard and contrary to human nature, a considerable number are of the opinion that happiness in life depends on casting aside the yoke anyway. On this pretext slaves of long ago were carried away by arrogance, as if they had been called to freedom by the preaching of the gospel; others used to exempt themselves from subjection to kings and magistrates. Similarly today, when a great many of the lowest order have tasted the gospel, they are insolent in the way they vaunt themselves: servants assume bold and high-minded attitudes, and not a few forget about propriety and discretion and arrogate to themselves whatever they please. But the worst aspect of it is that a great many people emancipate themselves from obeying God himself, just as if, in adopting us as sons, he deprived himself of every right and the authority belonging to a father. Certainly it is a horrible perversion and one that, by its baseness, can seriously wound all pious minds. But rather than our adding to it, let the vengeance of God consume us.

We are aware of what Isaiah has borne witness to concerning the gentleness of Christ (Isa. 42:2f.). We hear what Christ himself declares about himself: "Learn from me, for I am gentle and lowly in heart" (Matt. 11:29 — RSV). And the reason why Paul reminds us how, although he was "in the form of God, he emptied himself" (Phil. 2:6ff.), is that we may learn submission from him. When the Son of God descended from the throne of his heavenly majesty to the extent that he was clothed with our flesh, and submitted not only to the condition of a slave but also to the extreme ignominy of the cross (Phil. 2:6ff.), which one of us will not feel ashamed to be preening his feathers in order to be, or appear to be, something great? In order that they may conform to the example of the teacher, those who enjoy the greatest riches and honors and so stand above others must come down to the level of the lowly, as if they have forgotten their greatness. Therefore, if humble people use the gospel as an excuse to begin to give vent to lofty, overbearing spirits, their arrogance will be preposterous in the extreme. For the great will not be ordered to give up their right so that otherwise worthless men might usurp the right of others. Besides, this teaching not only lays down the principle of their duty to individuals, but also gives us plenty of correctives to 207 check the impudence of the arrogant; and at the same time it removes the reproach and blame for the evil from the gospel. Indeed, when poor men, who do not have the support of riches, influence, talent, or rank, obtrude themselves haughtily and contemptuously on others as soon as they have learned to chatter about the gospel, what else is to be expected but that such extremely bad behavior should irritate noble and prudent men? However, the silliness of the majority is so ridiculous that it ought to move us to shame and pity rather than provoke our indignation. Yet, are we to allow what offends us very much to exist, or will our indignation against stupid pride attack the actual source of all unassuming conduct?

Dissolute Lives

On the other hand, look at the many individuals who are dishonoring the profession of the gospel with dissolute and disgraceful lives. That gives rise to a scandal closely related to the last one. And certainly, in view of the fact that Paul asserts that we do honor to the gospel by leading "upright and godly lives" (Titus 2:12), those who take the liberty to indulge in bad living are so many reproaches and blemishes on Christianity. And indeed there is no doubt that the fearful vengeance of God waits for all such as dishonor the teaching of piety with their ungodly ways, and expose the sacred name of God to derision. One day they will realize what an intolerable offense it is to desecrate the sacred treasury of the gospel, and how it is not for nothing that it is said that "those who take his name in vain will not be held guiltless" (Exod. 20:7). They will realize how precious to God are the souls whom they shut out from the life of salvation by their own bad example. In the first place they are excessively audacious when, as Paul says, "they openly confess God with their lips but deny him by their deeds" (Titus 1:16), thus giving the impression that they are students of the heavenly wisdom when their whole life bespeaks plain contempt for God. But the fact that they take advantage of the gospel as a pretext for their enormities is sacrilegious impiety in the extreme. I am now[27] speaking about the common cunning by which treacherous and vile men worm their way in to deceive, defraud, and do harm in every possible way. In the past I have seen men who were not ashamed to make the gospel a cover and excuse for their pandering ways and filthy practices. Others are less corrupt, yet by their dissolute lives they pollute the Church with vices and cast a stigma on the gospel. Now, it is indeed an unfortunate and deplorable situation not only that the shameful deeds of men are being ascribed to the doctrine of holiness but also that it is being depreciated and disgraced in their persons.

Pastors' Dissolute Lives

But the Church has another ulcer that is more to be deplored: the fact that pastors — yes, I say the very pastors who mount the pulpit, which is the sacred judgment seat of Christ, on the condition that they surpass all others in the purity of their lives — are sometimes the most disgraceful examples of wantonness or other evils. So it turns out that their discourses possess no more truth and seriousness than if a player were acting out a tale on the stage. And, of course, such men complain that they are objects of contempt among the common

208

27. 1550 has, wrongly, "not" (*non*); changed to *iam*. [B-N]

people, or even that fingers are pointed at them as laughing-stocks. But rather am I surprised at the patience of the ordinary people, that women and children do not cover them with mud and filth. They boldly[28] exalt the dignity of the ministry, but it does not enter their heads that their esteem for the ministry is not accepted because they defile it by their own disgraceful conduct. Someone once truly said, "In order to be loved, be loving." In the same way those who wish to be appreciated need to gain respect by the seriousness and sanctity of their behavior. But I wish that the Church could be relieved and purged of dregs of men like these! But things usually turn out quite differently. For when they know that they themselves deserve contempt, their bad conscience deprives them of freedom. Indeed, they feel that their shameful deeds and lives make them obnoxious to all. Therefore, whenever grave action would be demanded, and because they themselves are no better, either they are held back by shame and fear and do not dare to open their mouths, or they are forced to let transgressors off and flatter them.

In addition, there are "idle gluttons" (Titus 1:12) who would allow heaven to be confounded with the earth, so that they may see to it that laws which are full of offense are valuable for their own leisure and pleasures. Some of them also, because they hate virtues, indulge in vices — other people's just as much as their own. On the other hand, the people — to show their gratitude — love, embrace, and support them, and, in order to have patrons for their pleasures, they look after those who give them their patronage. Yet at the same time they continually point to the scandal for themselves that arises from the corrupt life of the pastors, and they do so in order not to yield to Christ. That is indeed the height of perversity and impudence; but anyone who is kept back by the sin of men from coming to Christ does not deserve to be excused. It is just as if someone refuses to drink from a fountain because he says that it is choked with briers and thorns, when it is nevertheless possible to overcome the obstacles with little trouble and no danger. Because they see some who have the gospel on their lips leading vicious or

28. *Plenis buccis;* cf. p. 67, n. 25.

worthless lives they say, "There's the gospel for you!" How much better it would be were they to realize with sorrow how seriously God is hurt when a life responds so badly to the gospel! If the clouds cast a gloom over the earth, nobody is so mad or bold as to call the sun dark on that account. But there is the greatest difference between the brightness of the sun and the gospel. For although clouds may obscure the former, the depravity of men cannot prevent the splendor of the sound and godly doctrine shining through, so that, with the darkness driven away, our lives may be reshaped in true righteousness. Of course, we shall acknowledge that the sun is shining even when it lies hidden; but when we see the vivid light of the gospel and the glory of Christ refulgent in it, will the sins of men, whatever they may be in the end, dull our vision?

209

As far as leaders themselves are concerned, Christ already knew that it redounds very greatly to the dishonor of teaching if they lead unseemly lives. To avert this scandal he urges us to observe their actual instructions, although they do not touch, even with their little finger, the burdens that they lay on the shoulders of others (Matt. 23:3f.). At that time it was the duty of the scribes to give the people instruction in the law of God. But while they were interpreters of the divine law in the teacher's chair, at home and in the marketplace they were full of fraudulent ways, pride, cruelty, and perjuries; and they had the audacity to do anything that suited their own pleasure. Christ nevertheless means that his own authority from the Word of God remains intact. This admonition was not confined to that generation alone; on the contrary, today, whenever pastors lead a life that is inconsistent with their profession, the heavenly voice also cries in our ears that it is still wrong if this is a cause for disparaging the gospel in any way. Similarly, it is surely unworthy in the extreme to judge the rule that God has prescribed to enable us to live good lives by men's bad lives. One day indeed those men will have to give an account of themselves, and they will realize that it was not for nothing that it was said, "It would be better for a man to have a millstone hung about his neck now, and to be cast into the depths of the sea, rather than offend any single one of the very little ones"

(Mark 9:42). However, in the meantime it is our duty to hasten to the goal by the way that the Lord has prepared for us.

Personal Injury

However, the scandal is doubled whenever private injury is added to vile sins. When some have been given generous hospitality, they either depart in secret loaded with stolen goods, or defraud their hosts in other ways, or seduce the maidservants, and sometimes even dare to lead the wives astray. Others, who are past masters at taking people in, leave those to whom they promised wealth in abundance stripped bare. Others default on a loan; others again refuse something entrusted to them; while others are dishonest with their business associates. Others have taken money from good and honest men, pretending it was for alms, and spend it either in fornication, dicing, or other extravagances and debaucheries. Others brazenly devour in idleness what had been given by way of a loan to help them in their business. And some have their wives in league with them for those disgraceful practices. Others have no hesitation about violating the most sacred bond of marriage, deceiving their wives, and casting their children aside. Instead of citing more examples of such misdeeds, let this brief catalogue suffice. Certainly the treachery of those men can only have the effect of inflicting a serious and bitter wound on upright spirits. Indeed, it is bound to be the case that good men who have very little property should be alarmed when they see themselves stripped, as if they had fallen into the hands of robbers, and reduced to poverty — and all on the pretext of the gospel.

210

And we must bear in mind something that is among our harder exercises, that we are urged to take note of those who mock at the gospel in this way, and with impunity at that. Certainly, if God — speaking through Paul — justifiably forbids us to grow weary of doing good to many, even though we know from experience that they are ungrateful and vicious (II Thess. 3:13), and he does so in order that by our acts of kindness we may not neglect anyone who is in genuine need, we must be

73

all the more careful to be on our guard so that the perversity of men does not drive us to such a state of peevishness that we are ungrateful and disobedient to God. Therefore, on the one hand we ought to keep a sharp lookout, that there may be no opportunity for such scoundrels to do harm. We must resist their stratagems, and as far as it is our concern we must take care that their frauds and wrongs are severely punished by the magistrates, and that those to whom the Word of God is a laughingstock, and who insolently mock at the Church, may meet their deserts by having the hangman for a teacher and the gallows for a school. Again, on the other hand, we must guard against the crafty devices of Satan much more strictly lest, when he has brought about the loss of our perishable wealth, he might tear the heavenly treasure out of our hands. For he tries to do that, and that is something far more deadly for us. "Anyone who has hope in Christ purifies himself" (I John 3:3). When we know that those who do not aspire to this purity plead the name of Christ falsely, as an excuse, why then are they hindering us and keeping us back by their depravity? The gospel is indeed the bread of life, but it is by no means the case that all digest it; for though many seem to swallow it greedily, few of them know the taste of it. Finally, when Christ compares his Church to a threshing floor (Matt. 3:12)[29] where the wheat is mixed up with the chaff, so that it mostly lies hidden and buried under it, he is likening to the chaff not those who are outside but those who take a place among believers on a false profession of the gospel. Why else would he also have declared that on the Last Day he will not know many who will boast that they were preachers of the gospel, and protest that miracles were performed by them (Matt. 7:22f.), except that some people like that must appear in every generation?

The Failure of God-fearing Men

It sometimes also happens that those who otherwise fear God sincerely, or at any rate are not false through and through,

---

29. The speaker is, of course, not Christ but John the Baptist. [tr.]

fall into some horrible crime and bring disgrace both on themselves and the pure religion that they follow. When David
yielded to his lust and seized another man's wife, what a
disgraceful business that was! For not only did he pour out the
innocent blood of the one man who deserved well of David
himself, but he also brought ruin on all God's people, just as
much as on himself (II Sam. 11ff.). If one likes to list scandals of
this kind which could alarm heroes, think of the monstrous
crimes that the blessed patriarch Jacob saw in his household.
After his daughter had been forced, Simeon and Levi carried 211
out a slaughter with a cruelty that was just as barbaric as the
abominable treachery of Shechem (Gen. 34). Imbued with
murder, his sons plotted together to kill their brother (Gen. 37).
The incestuous lying of his first-born with his stepmother is
added to the accumulation of evils.[30] And yet the Church of
God was at that time limited to one house. I refrain from citing
more examples.

Today indeed some will investigate a few scandals with
eagle eye,[31] in order not to have any association with the whole
Church of God, wherever it makes its appearance. I am content to have used this one example to warn my readers that faith
will be exceedingly unstable if it gives way immediately at the
downfall of individual men. At any rate, this must be held as an
axiom, that it undoubtedly happens according to the purpose of
God that evil men are always mixed up with good. In this way
the firmness of faith is put to the test, we are disciplined in
patience, the zeal for prayer is kindled, the pricks of difficulties
cause us to walk cautiously and prudently, contempt for the
world arises, and, along with the desire to depart, meditation
on the life of heaven grows. Even if the reason be hidden, let
us realize, however, that part of our warfare consists of those
exercises, and we must be involved in that warfare through
the whole course of our life.

---

30. *Noverca. B-N* quotes Gen. 38 (see vv. 12-19), which suits chronologically but
refers to Judah and his daughter-in-law. For Reuben, the actual first-born,
and his father's concubine, see Gen. 35:22f.; cf. *Inst.,* II, x, 12; IV, i, 24. [tr.]
31. Lit. "with the eye of Lynceus," who was an Argonaut famous for his sharp
sight. [tr.]

Fickleness

A great deal of harm is also done by the fickleness that is seen everywhere in very many people. After they begin by showing astonishing ardor the flame vanishes so quickly that one might say it came from flax. Although others may have intended to hold fast all the way through, yet they cool off gradually. The ignorant ascribe to repentance what is due in part to vanity, in part to laziness, and in part to worldly cares. Therefore, they themselves also draw back at an early stage so as not to repent too late of having gone too far. If any of them abandon the gospel because they are terrified by the fear of death or persecutions (something that happens to many, I am sorry to say), their inconstancy is made the grounds of a scandal. Their failure is certainly disgraceful. But no matter how all of us may deny Christ, will he deny himself for that reason? On the contrary, he will remain above reproach and perpetually self-consistent notwithstanding, as Paul also reminds us (II Tim. 2:13). Examples like these should have had quite a different effect on us, namely, that having been made aware of our weakness, we took good care that the same thing did not happen to us. After Paul has recounted that the Jews have been cut off from the grace of God, he shows that their calamity is so terrible that he strongly urges and encourages others to be on their guard (Rom. 11:17-24). Therefore, if those whose anxiety ought to be aroused by entire peoples departing from the gospel are alarmed by the desertion of this or that individual, may we not put the blame down to their perverse judgment?

212   Yet it is not my purpose to minimize the offense of those who, as far as they are responsible, cause weak souls to waver. Only I wish those who totter with others who are falling to be warned how malicious their consternation is. "This man has denied Christ. Who would have thought it? That man, whom everybody used to believe firmer than a rock, has taken farewell of the gospel. This one is lukewarm already, another is colder than ice, when they seemed marvelous in keeping up a burning enthusiasm." But those who talk like that do not consider that some are crushed by the fear of death because they have not yet laid hold of the firm hope of eternal life, and that others are

dull because the empty cares of the world stifle the glow of the Spirit in them.

But why should we voluntarily assist in summoning infectious disease from others to ourselves when a remedy is readily available, except that we refuse it? Why do we not rather acquiesce in this admonition of Paul that is so salutary? For after speaking about Hymenaeus and Philetus, whose error could produce great alarm in all the believers, he at once suggests something of value for strengthening them. "This seal remains, The Lord knoweth them that are his. Therefore, let everyone who invokes the name of the Lord depart from unrighteousness" (II Tim 2:17-19). Since these two were well-known, celebrated figures, Paul sees that their downfall is bound to have the effect of persuading others at least to waver. However, he encourages the elect to rest securely on the protection of God, and he says that there is no danger that the seal of salvation, engraved by him, will ever be destroyed. At the same time he warns against anyone profaning the Holy Name of God by a false invocation. John also was undoubtedly aware of this scandal from those who were doing powerful harm to the Church in his day by spreading the poison of ungodly doctrine. But while asserting that this happens, so that it might be made manifest that all who arrogate the name to themselves are not of the company of the godly (I John 2:19), at the same time he is pointing out the method of surmounting that scandal, which could hinder quite a number of people. What about Alexander the coppersmith? Since he had become a deserter from the celebrated disciple of Christ, and then his most bitter enemy, is he not set before others as an example (II Tim. 4:14)? What of Demas? When, "having loved this present world," he basely abandoned the gospel, should he have drawn others into the same labyrinth with himself (II Tim. 4:10)? When, in another verse, Paul remembers that "all forsook" him, does he give others the liberty to give up the gospel (II Tim. 4:16)? When he complains that he was thrown aside by "Phygelus, Hermogenes and all who are in Asia," is he giving other people the opportunity to tear themselves away as infamously (II Tim. 1:15)? On the contrary, all the godly are alerted by examples such as these so that their security may not be exposed to the crafty devices of Satan. They are commanded so to set that perpetual seal of divine election against all attacks by way of a shield that they also seal their faith with a good conscience [II Tim. 2:19; I Tim. 1:19].

213 Since it is my concern to deal with those men who wish to be reckoned as Christians, and so that the discussion of this matter may not be drawn out too far, let them read the two letters of Paul to Timothy. For, in my opinion, these will more than suffice for giving them peace of mind; unless perhaps, after they have given these letters their attention, they are either eager in their desire to put themselves in a state of great confusion or deliberately snatch at empty excuses for separating themselves from Christ. For reasonable and prudent men this one thing will certainly be fitting for sustaining faith, that it is wrong for us to measure the eternal truth of God by the changing inconstancy of men. But why do those who are so skilful at letting bad examples give them opportunity to indulge in sin not take note of so many wonderful examples of invincible constancy, which could deservedly strengthen faith in the midst of stormy temptations of all kinds? This generation of ours has seen a goodly number of martyrs going to their deaths eagerly and fearlessly. And this glory was not restricted to men, but God has let us see women possess a strength that was more than manly. Certainly the old histories honor no women of discernment [*cordatas*] who are not matched by those whom Flanders and the province of Artois have produced these last ten years.[32] Therefore, will the treacherous desertion of certain individuals overthrow our faith? Will that sacred blood, the separate drops of which are so many seals to believing hearts, vanish away[33] as valueless and ineffective? Even if it is worthless to those people, yet it will not be inglorious to God. They indeed will not get off with impunity for having voluntarily joined themselves as companions of ruin to the deserters of Christ, and certainly for having neglected those who call us to heaven with outstretched hands.

32. *Flandria et Artesii comitatus.* B-N refers to Jean Crespin, *Histoire des vrays Tesmoins* (1570), II, 95ff.: "Les martyrs de Louvain, 1540." *Bulletin de la Société de l'histoire du Protestantisme français* (Paris), V, 562.
33. Reading *evanescet* for *avanescet*. [tr.]

Dissensions: Reformed and Roman

I come to that obstacle which has prevented many people in our time from coming closer to Christ. For they have seen the leading teachers of the renascent gospel not only disagreeing among themselves with their opposing viewpoints but even engaging in bitter conflicts. Here the doubt has invaded their minds about how much confidence was to be had in those disagreeing at the beginning. The fear has also arisen that they might rashly advance to a position from which they could not draw back. In particular, it need hardly be said how much that unhappy controversy about the sacraments disturbed many people's minds.[34] I myself have experienced to my own cost how remarkable Satan's artifice has been in creating resistance in timid consciences. But since I afterwards realized that I was hindered more by my own fault than held back by a reasonable cause, I am not afraid to say the same thing about others. Indeed, I grant that there is something about dissensions of this kind that dishearten those already to some extent established, not to speak of the ignorant and beginners; but I maintain that they must recover their courage so that they may nevertheless continue to come to him who is never sought in vain. For there is no deception about his promise: "it shall be opened if we knock; it shall be given if we ask" (Matt. 7:8).

There is not the slightest excuse for those who, out of hatred   214
for the dissensions which they have seen on our side, boast that they still adhere to the teaching of the papacy. I am speaking about something which is quite notorious. There is not a principle of religion about which those with a taste for theology do not contend every day in that quarter. Granted that there may be opposite opinions, yet their books bear witness to the odious way they both condemn and violently attack each other. Even more, they consider that it is a glorious thing for them to acknowledge different schools [*sectas*]. Accordingly, the innumerable quarrels and fights of the papists are no offense to those good men, while a single dissension among us hurts them so much that they shrink back at once from the whole of our teaching. Of course, there is one thing in which the papists

34. *Inst.*, IV, xvii.

are very much in agreement, for they all eagerly prattle against the gospel, and defend their own impious superstitions with as much clamor as obstinacy. But when they revert to themselves, they shout at each other in turn with nothing else but raucous and confused garrulity. Of course, I know that monks and chatterers of the same breed are so corrupt and impudent that they prevent the common folk from tasting the gospel, mainly with the excuse that we do not agree well among ourselves. As if indeed the walls of the schools do not resound with their internal battles! As if all their books are not crammed full of fighting sentiments, as I have said! However, I am not surprised that those people to whom a deplorable audacity is the highest virtue behave so insolently. But how does it really come about that men with eyes in their heads, and who are well aware of all the things about which I am speaking, pretend to be moved by an argument of this kind? Is it not that they deliberately avoid the light? And in that situation they make a great song about their wisdom in not involving themselves in dangerous disputes; indeed, they laugh at others who still dare to seek after the way of salvation, as if they are not cautious enough. Since I know no better remedy for correcting the pride of those men than contempt, I turn to simpler people who, conscious of their own ignorance, prefer to abstain from studying to seek after the truth rather than suffer the danger of going wrong.

The Lord's Supper

After Luther on the one hand, and Oecolampadius and Zwingli on the other, were successful in their strenuous efforts to re-establish the rule of Christ, there arose that unhappy dispute about the Holy Supper of the Lord, and a great many others have been drawn into association with them. It must be more a source of grief than surprise that that conflict among the foremost leaders causes alarm to overtake beginners. However, so that these same beginners may not be unduly perturbed, they must be warned that it is an old trick of Satan's to rush otherwise prudent servants of God into controversies with each other so that he may hinder the course of sound doctrine. Who

wishes to yield of his own accord to Satan's crafty ways? Thus
Paul's quarrel with Barnabas reached a violent climax (Acts
15:39). Thus Paul's similar disagreement with Peter broke out   215
into open conflict (Gal. 2:11). In the case of those three men
everyone recognizes what I have mentioned — the stratagem of
Satan. In the present situation, when it is a question of their
own salvation, why are they blind? Someone will object that
those were not controversies about doctrine. Why? When certain
men were pressing the ceremonies of the Mosaic law, was not
this a question of doctrine (Gal. 2:12)? Yet the split was
carried so far that it rent nearly all the churches. Or will they say
that it was right for the gospel to be rejected on account of that
disturbance?

It is well known that Luther and those with whom he dis-
agreed were prudent men, equipped with singular gifts of God.
They were all in remarkable agreement about the whole substance of the faith. They were unanimous in their teaching
about what the proper and sincere worship of God should be,
and they endeavored to cleanse it of countless superstitions and
idolatries and to free it from the corrupt inventions of men.
They rejected reliance on works, by which men had been intoxicated and indeed bewitched, and taught the restoration of
total salvation in the grace of Christ. They have magnificently
lifted up the virtue of Christ, after it had either fallen and lain
prostrate or been submerged and hidden from view. Those
men do not differ in their teaching about what is the true
method of invocation, what is the nature and essence of penitence from which faith arises and produces certain fruits, and
what is the legitimate government of the Church. Only on the
symbols themselves was there any disagreement. Yet I deliberately venture to assert that, if their minds had not been partly
exasperated by the extreme vehemence of the controversies,
and partly possessed by wrong suspicions, the disagreement
was not so great that conciliation could not easily have been
achieved. Even if, because of the vehemence of that dispute,
the controversy could not have been resolved properly, is there
anything to prevent the plain truth being heard at least now, as
in the calm after the storm?

We are all very much in agreement about what the true use of the sacraments is. We all teach in common that the sacraments have been instituted in order that they may seal the promises of God to our hearts, that they may be supports for our faith and testimonies of the divine grace. We clearly point out that they are not empty or bare and dead forms [*figuras*] since their use is efficacious by the power of the Holy Spirit; and by the secret virtue of the Holy Spirit, God is really offering everything that he shows in them. So we acknowledge that the bread and wine in the Holy Supper are not empty pledges of that communication which believers have with Christ,[35] their head, because our souls enjoy him as spiritual nourishment.[36] Everywhere there is agreement about the teaching on all these points. Why then do proud men find such a stumbling block in this connection that it bars the way to the gospel?

Someone may object, however, that in defining the mode the theory [*ratio*] is somewhat diverse. I certainly admit that all do not speak as clearly as one would wish, whether because they do not all have the same skill for clear and lucid expression or because they have not all acquired the same measure of faith. Since much of the dense darkness of the papacy is still left, if anyone is annoyed that everything serving to scatter the darkness of errors is carefully and plainly set forth, he is revealing that he is shunning the light maliciously. But when we, for our part, lift up men from earth to heaven; when we transfer them from the elements of death to Christ; when we place the ground of righteousness, salvation, and all good things in his pure grace; when we attribute the whole efficacy of the signs to the Holy Spirit, and inasmuch as God is the sole author and perfecter of the spiritual life, we claim totally for him what belongs to him; when we repudiate all the stupid fictions by which the world has plainly been deceived; when we do away with the physical mode of the presence of Christ and the wrongful adoration of him in the sign — when those who imagine a stumbling block in all those things are knowingly and willingly stumbling over Christ, they deserve to bruise themselves. I know by experience in this cause that there are indeed many

216

35. *Ibid.*, IV, xvii, 1.
36. *Ibid.*, IV, xvii, 3.

who are helped by the pretext of scandals, because it suits them to be blind in the midst of light.

Alleged Errors

In addition we must recall what I touched on briefly earlier.[37] Since new situations give an opportunity for many wrong steps, if any mistake is then made, stricter attention is paid to it and it is more severely condemned than if no change had been made. We remember with amazement how deep was the whirlpool of ignorance and how horrible the darkness of errors in the papacy. Then it was a great miracle of God that Luther and those who labored at the same time in restoring the doctrine of the faith were able to extricate themselves from it little by little. Some pretend that they are offended because they did not see everything all at once and because such a difficult task was not brought to absolute perfection on the first day, and they do so in order not to give their assent to the gospel or to complete the course after starting out on it. Who does not see how irrelevant those splendid ideas are? For it is exactly as if someone finds fault with us because at the first streak of dawn we do not yet see the midday sun. Nothing is more familiar than these complaints. "Why has it not been laid down for us once and for all what we ought to follow?" "Why has this, rather than other things, been concealed?" "Will there ever be any end if permission is continually being given to aim at something further?" Of course, those who speak like that either begrudge the servants of God their success or are annoyed that the Kingdom of Christ is being advanced to a better state. The same peevish spirit is apparent in regard to all the most trifling errors; yet, even if these do not deserve to be overlooked altogether, they ought not to provoke us to a dislike of the gospel. The monks and other teachers of the papal synagogue[38] may babble their futile dirges as much as they like, they may disfigure Scripture with absurd glosses to their hearts' content, yet those good fellows have no difficulty about condoning it all. If   217

37. See p. 13 above.
38. "He is referring to those of the Sorbonne, according to the French version." [B-N]

our men put out something that is perhaps not quite appropriate, they pretend they are kept back from hearing us as if by a great crime. They patiently put up with obscure scriptural testimonies, contradictory opinions, and frivolous themes in the ancient writers; but if they find one percent of them in the writings of our men, not only will they condemn all of us who will be innocent but they will consider keeping the whole of doctrine at arm's length. However, this is not the place for me to undertake the defense of those who relieve their own itching with a desire to write. For one would wish that people like that would refrain from corrupting their writings. But while, on the one hand, I concede that the follies of a few men must not be encouraged by complacence, on the other hand, all see how unjust it is that the whole doctrine of the gospel is rendered tasteless by this disgust. What I have said is indeed true, that those things that previously lay hidden as if in the darkness of night are seen far more clearly in the full light of the gospel. But on the one hand cheerfully and unconcernedly conniving at any errors you like, while on the other hand paying very particular attention to the things at which you carp, is, I maintain, indeed the mark of those who are eagerly on the lookout for imaginary scandals for themselves.

Dissolute Lives: Charge and Countercharge

Now the only stumbling block that really arises for those people is the one provided for them by certain men whose lives do not correspond to what they profess. If it were just a case of the corrupt and dissolute lives of those who boast that they follow the gospel, that could be regarded as quite a plausible cause for a stumbling block. But since crimes have been sweeping indiscriminately through almost the whole world, must we not say that the ancient complaint of the poet is just as apposite to our own times also? "Our fathers in their day were morally poorer than our grandfathers; but they begot us who are still worse, and soon we shall produce children who will be even more corrupt."[39] And what is the purpose of Christ's warning

39. Horace, *Odes*, III, vi, 46ff.

84

that the last times will be like the age of Noah, with some fearful flood of wickedness which will overwhelm the earth (Luke 17:26f.), except that such a filthy conflux of crimes may quicken the desire to make haste to Christ, along with those already hurrying to him of their own accord? To this is also to be added the just avenging of the despised gospel, as I have already mentioned.[40] For who may say that those who abuse such a sacred treasure do not deserve it when the Lord drives them into a reprobate state of mind, so that they prostitute themselves to every kind of shameful deed? And indeed nothing else is to be expected than that everywhere men grow more and more profane, when we know that there are few who do not share in that particular sacrilege.

However, to the reasons given above I add this other one: those who are held back from the gospel by the faults of our men are malicious and unfair critics. They say that very many who glory in the gospel behave neither piously nor honestly, and the first thing that had to be asked was if the gospel has changed them for the worse. "The man who was a fornicator," they say, "or a gambler, or dissolute in some other way, is exactly the same today."[41] Indeed, the very vices they tolerate in the papacy they suddenly begin to detest so much that in their hatred of them they also stand in horror of the doctrine of holiness and uprightness itself. I have no fear of those who bring disgrace on the gospel by their unseemly and dissolute lives thinking that I shall come to their defense. And that means that I shall have greater freedom, in my own opinion, to rebuke those who ascribe to the gospel all the corruptions of the papacy. 218

If any holiness is sought there, the monks arrogate it to themselves, with everyone agreeing and no controversy about it. Why may they not do so when angelic perfection resides in their cloisters? Rather, no other place provides us with a fouler collection of all the vices. If anyone objects that, since only infected things issue from there, it is no wonder if they give off a stench wherever they come, it is easy to put an end to such a silly cavil. For in the first place, if there was anything good

---

40. See pp. 59 ff., 69-70 above.
41. "In particular he is referring to Philip the Landgrave of Hesse." [B-N]

there, it is certain that it would have been brought forth by the wonderful providence of God — like gold out of a refuse heap. What monks has Germany had in our day who may dare to compare themselves either in doctrine or holiness with Luther, Bucer, Oecolampadius, and men like them, unless they are impudent in the extreme? Whom may the Italians set against Bernardino Ochino and Peter Vermigli?[42] From the brothels of France also have issued forth some who by their own excellence concealed the many disgraceful and infamous things of their own order. Certainly I grant that few have crossed over to us from the monkhood who deserve to be mentioned out of respect. And what wonder if few angels emerge from the infernal regions? We are right to ascribe the escape of one man, Lot, from Sodom in safety to the extraordinary power of God (Gen. 19:12ff.). But what Sodom was ever crammed with so many filthy monstrosities as today swarm in the brothels of the monks? Therefore, I am accustomed to say that if only a tenth part of those who fly out of those places in the name of Christianity were truly to devote themselves to Christ, we should be doing very well. On the contrary, every day we see Christ being defrauded of his tithes, so that scarcely five percent come to him.

But I say that those who provide the opportunity for a scandal are not so much perverse by nature and infamous because of their own personal crimes as they are infected by the filthy and abominable education of the monkhood. For seeing that they are idle gluttons, quarrelsome, treacherous, ungrateful, devoid of human kindness, power-seeking, thievish, servile by temperament, and libidinous, do not all these things smack of the cloistered way of life? Indeed, their different orders have their own separate and distinct rules, yet they all usually possess a common rule fused from those "virtues" [*virtutibus*] which I have listed. For if the best men whom the Lord pulled out of that filth know that the infection contracted from it sticks so tenaciously that it must be their daily task to wipe away the remains of it, one can imagine how much the contagion attacks the common herd. Therefore, let those who

219

42. Bernardino Ochino (1487-1564) became a Protestant under the influence of Peter Martyr (Pietro Martire Vermigli, 1500-62). See *ODCC*, pp. 990, 1073f.

are held back by scandals of this kind accept what their responsibility is, and they will find the way plain and consistent. Indeed, if I had the power of the magistrate and money in large enough supply to keep up the expense of it, I should set free the monk after he has left his cell, but only for a minimum of six months and after he has been tested by a strict examination, so that he might enjoy the common life and society of men; and all whom I should see still clothed in their monkishness I should shut up in a penitentiary or remove like wild animals to some forest. Besides, to wash away the filth from the papacy, where it clearly belongs, and to throw it back on the name of the gospel is a thorough misrepresentation.

But why am I discussing what appears on one side? For if the papists reproach us with a dissolute life because the behavior of some people is far from respectable, we may with perfect justice retort that they have the same shameful things, and even twice as many. If only they would provide us with less abundant material! No useful purpose is served in telling how much fornication goes on among them with impunity, how free they are to indulge in quarreling and fighting, how lascivious practices of ever kind are allowed, how uninhibited shows, immodest dances, and other things of the same order hold sway and are loudly applauded. There is certainly not one of these things which — I may reasonably boast — is not forbidden among us by public decrees and held in check by some discipline. That is why there is no fear of our being compared with the papists and found equally disgraceful. It is because we take stock of our evils that we are filled with great shame. But it is a lamentable fact that the extreme filthiness of those men causes us to appear quite virtuous and blameless. It is thus extraordinary that those who are so fastidious about putting up with the vices of our men are twice as inflexible in their toleration of the crimes of the opposite side. In that way they not only cause us injury but are also most ungrateful to God. For at the same time they are neglecting a great many examples of rare piety, holiness, and all the virtues; and they ought to be quickened by these to love and reverence the gospel rather than moved to hatred and contempt of it by the misdeeds of some men. They plead as an excuse that many have not come to their senses after surrendering to the gospel. But, in fact, how many from the opposite side can one bring forward whose wonderful conversion does honor to our gospel?

And since those who obscure the glory of the gospel so maliciously force us to boast, there is no region which may not see every day the magnificent triumphs of our teaching in this respect. Also, our adversaries themselves, no matter what they pretend, are nevertheless torn by frenzy, because they see men who had previously been devoted to intemperance, licentious practices, unchastity, the vain shows of the world, avarice, and robbery, now restored to sobriety, continence, chastity, unassuming behavior, and fair dealing. But if you are looking for people whose lives have been consistently virtuous and of excellent reputation all the way through, we also have a considerable number of them. I should be quite able to name many who were once outstanding and held in the highest esteem in the papacy and who, since they were granted a pure knowledge of the gospel by God, now show, by portraying a living image of the virtues in their lives, that they had only a shadow of them before. But so that this discussion may not be offensive through giving rather an impression of boastfulness, I shall conclude it briefly, if examples may persuade any. The remarkable piety demonstrated in death as well as life, the righteousness, chastity, and temperateness of both men and women ought to confirm faith far more effectively than any justification there may be for the disordered lives of others doing harm to it.

PART III: THE THIRD CLASS OF SCANDALS: "EXTRINSIC"

LET US NOW PASS to the last class of scandals. As I have said,[1] this partly consists of fictitious calumnies and partly arises from malicious insults, which — far-fetched though they be — perverted men unjustly turn against the gospel.

Calumnies: From False Teachers

As far as calumnies are concerned I should like to say first of all that there is no cause for wonder if, by spreading them far and wide, ungodly men are endeavoring to subvert the trustworthiness of our teaching among simple people. And indeed it is not right that we should be exempt from the principle that normally affects the servants of God. Certainly, Paul was not so peevish as to have no good reason for giving vent to those complaints which are to be found all through his writings. He was silent about many things by virtue of his own sagacity, he overlooked many things on account of his own moderation, he swallowed many things in silence because of his own greatness of mind; and yet we see how often he complains that he has been treated shamefully and hatefully by the churches. I am speaking about the underhand way spiteful men took advantage of Paul's absence and unawareness to heap disparagements on him among people who were exceedingly credulous

1.   See p. 14 above.

and ignorant of the true state of affairs. For it is quite well known that the servants of God, and even the Son himself, have been openly attacked by obvious calumnies. It is true that when Satan sees that he is getting nowhere with open warfare, he makes covert attacks on the reputation of the pious as if by burrowing underground. Accordingly, when Paul was engaged in a stern warfare in remote regions, when he was striving to extend the Kingdom of Christ through a thousand hazards, when he was constantly clashing with many different enemies, when he was running hither and thither in his concern to gather into the unity of the faith nations who were far apart from one another — in other places cowardly and worthless whisperers were burdening him with unworthy crimes. When even Paul's integrity was not able to protect him, who among us may demand that his reputation be untouched by every malicious attack that wicked men can make? On the contrary, because he testifies that he did so, let us carry on with unbroken courage "through evil and good report" (II Cor. 6:8).

221   For it is just as necessary for the servants of Christ to despise sinister rumors as to keep well away from the worthless snares of vainglory. For Satan seeks to entrap them by adding this burden to adverse opinions, so that he might crush or at least check their eagerness for doing what is right. Besides, since it is not at all fitting for us to be upset every time our doing well brings bad reports to our ears, so it is only those who are troubled by their own guilt who show themselves unduly credulous by listening to whispers and false accusations. How many tales have Luther's enemies told about him throughout the whole of twenty-five years in public debates and published books! There are no monstrous lies which they have not ventured to concoct and babble against us. Picartus,[2] the teacher in Paris, is certainly mentally disturbed and even fanatical, but he has such a great reputation among his own people that all his dirges are regarded as undoubted oracles. While ranting in his usual way on the platform, he has ventured to say that we now absolutely deny that there is any God. And that fellow is certainly well aware that he is lying shamelessly; but because men

2.   For 16th-century references, see *B-N*.

90

like that have made up their minds to attack us in any way they can, they think that they have the right to blab about us anything that can stir up ill will against us. And, of course, when they already know very well that they have no reason for doing so unless it be to make fools of the wretched multitude along with themselves, it is no wonder that they abuse the refuge that they really need. But whatever they may have been disposed to invent for themselves, even without excuse, it ought not to have gained the credence it has straightaway. It is, however, such a common thing that it is even looked upon as lawful. If I were to recall all the stupid and ridiculous nonsense that they have uttered about me, the danger is that I may involve myself in their absurdities. I merely say this: if it be established as a law among us that the more unrestrained and shameless the lies of our enemies be the worse the cause of the gospel may be, and its credibility decline by the same extent, it is not because such hostile judges complain that a scandal is put in their way but because they show that they desire it of their own accord. But we may be permitted to say fearlessly with Paul, "If any man is ignorant let him be ignorant" (I Cor. 14:38).

Calumnies: From Rogues

I come to a second kind of disparagement. This not only emerges from the same workshop of Satan, but is also fashioned upon almost the same anvil. The only difference is that, whereas those men of whom I have just spoken are open and professed enemies, bringing the gospel into disrepute in their ministries among the common people, those concerning whom I am about to speak insinuate themselves in the name of the gospel so that by indirect whispers they may alienate whomever they can from Christ. Those people in fact consist partly of hungry vagabonds who, unless you fill their bellies, will bury you under wagonloads of calumnies, partly of 222 worthless and vicious men who, having been dismissed by us because of their own fault, or even having resigned from some office on account of a crime, seek out fresh pastures elsewhere; yet for both, the mind and tongue are in the belly. There are others a little better off, considering that they are not so pressed by hunger; yet, because they avoid the cross and desire an excuse for their own cowardice, cover over the pure expression of the gospel with heaps of tales invented by themselves. I have already said a little earlier[3] that an enormous number of drones are wandering about bent on stealing or cheating. Since their impostures are already so well known that they find no further opportunity for deception in the churches of Christ, they have therefore gone off elsewhere and impudently blab out anything they like against us in order to gain favor for themselves and hatred for us among the ignorant. But why do good men, who find a scandal in the vanity of those men, object to us?

We see monks who are indolent and yet accustomed to satisfy their gluttony, so that unless food is put into their mouths they soon burn "to sanctify war," as the prophet says (Mic. 3:5).[4] We also see others not unlike the monks. They all promise that they will be semi-angels if only a bearable way of life falls to their lot, and that they will be content with bread and water. But that show of endurance soon vanishes into thin air. In fact, after they have given a brief example of their sloth, disgusted with the hard work, they take their flight in secret. I certainly admit that many go away when they have sought in vain for the conditions they desire, as must necessarily happen when there is a great concourse of applicants. Indeed, I can well believe that some people who might be more deserving of assistance are yet sometimes given rather niggardly help, either because it is not possible to make a careful choice out of unknown men, or because those who are bolder about asking forestall the timid and diffident, or because we do not always make the right decision, or because — already impoverished by what we have paid out — we are forced to send away those who come at unsuitable times, either empty-handed or at least poorly aided. And yet wherever they go, the latter, who might have a better excuse, are rather moderate and cautious in what they say. The complaints of the former fly everywhere.

And what are the complaints like? They are full of prodigious lies. Those who were either driven from our midst by

---

3. See pp. 73-74 above.
4. Lit. "to make holy war" (*ad sanctificandum praelium*); cf. *Vulg., sanctificant . . . praelium; RV* mgn., "to sanctify." *RV* has "prepare war." [tr.]

their own crimes, or were alienated in treacherous defection, are even now more outrageous in the way they slander us when they chase after the favor of the rich with calumnies, so that they may stuff[5] their bellies by licking the latter's dishes. For it is no secret that many are to be found[6] who would like a gospel for themselves that is undisturbing and completely trouble-free. This is because they are ashamed to face up to the truth, that fear of the cross is hindering them from making a satisfactory Christian profession. Those people are very eager to find out if there are any vices in the churches of Christ, so that they may not appear to be attached to their own nests without a good reason. "Certainly," they say, "if the false show of idolatry is to be condemned in us, the fact nevertheless remains that people are also committing sins elsewhere in different ways." And yet they are seeking a pretext from lies which, it is certain, scoundrels of that sort invent to please them.

223

I should like to mention two or three examples, so that in the future no one may be deceived knowingly and willingly. There was a certain Corteis, a minister of the Word in the region of Montbéliard.[7] After he was driven out of there, he withdrew to Neuchâtel. When he had a colder reception there than he had hoped for, in order to avenge himself — and helped by the agency of certain people like himself — he caused many severe troubles for the godly brethren. Still, realizing in the end that he was powerless, and — what is a common thing with foxes of that sort — seeking forgiveness humbly, not only did he appease the offended brethren with a deceptive show of penitence, but when he was making out that he was in doubt about several questions, he obtained letters to me in which they asked in a friendly way that I might try to give him satisfaction. I asked the man to a meal and listened patiently, with the result that he declared with many tears that all his difficulties had now

---

5. "1550 wrongly reads *reficiant;* amended to *referciant.*" [B-N]
6. *Inveniri,* lacking in 1550. [B-N]
7. Or Cortèse; Latin name: *Courtesius.* For *in Comitatu Monsbergardensi,* "le pays de Montbéliard" (Mömpelgard), see *CR,* XI, Letter 534. Letter 498: "He was a minister of the Word in the village of Villars, near Blamont, in the region of Montbéliard (*in Comitatu Monsbergardensi*)." B-N refers to eight other letters in *CR,* XI. Montbéliard is in France, south of Belfort, and west of Basel. [tr.]

been removed. I also provided him with money when he set out on a journey. Thereafter, as he moved here and there through France, he never ceased reviling me in an impudent way.

There was another man, whose native land I do not know, but who had given himself the name of de Cornoz.[8] When he had been accused of doing some things unworthy of a servant of Christ, he was ordered by a judgment of the Synod of Lausanne to desist from his ministry until his case was more fully investigated. Not long afterwards he was carrying letters to Bern. Suspecting that they were not written to his liking, he replaced them with others. When he realized that the disgraceful deed was discovered, he was not able to avoid being branded with fraud, and so he secured his escape elsewhere on foot. All these things happened in my absence and without my knowledge. Now he maintains that he was driven out with violence by me because he refused to subscribe to my heresies.

Another, who had been rebuked by us because he spent too much time in taverns, never gave up secret revelings until the power of foreign air subdued him. When he left his family and hurried away in secret, I had set out for Strasbourg. There was no disagreement between us and no suggestion of antipathy. The only thing was that for a short time I had withstood him to prevent his going to ruin. But because he belonged to the herd of the Augustinians, he was wandering through the caves of his fellows, mournfully relating that he was living in exile because he too had opposed my heresies.

I am really not complaining so much about the villainy of him and those like him, but rather I am annoyed by the mean behavior of good fathers who, although they learn from our books every day, do not hesitate, on account of a bribe, to make a great fuss about scandals derived from those lapses. But it is foolish of me to employ both my readers and myself in listing those riffraff, were it not that it was necessary that there be represented, so to speak, in the characters of a few men what is

224

8. Letter of the Ministers of Geneva to the Consistory of Bern, 31 August, 1537: "Several of those refugees were established pastors in French Switzerland. Among others we can cite . . . Jean de Cornoz, who was sent into a parish in the district of Gex." This is the only place where the name de Cornoz is found. B-N gives reference in Herminjard, IV, 288. Gex is in France near the Swiss border and Geneva. [tr.]

usually done by very many people everywhere and every day.

To others we are exceedingly inflexible and implacable. But it is worthwhile investigating what sort of clemency they ask of us. When we are unjustly injured we pardon, and we do not take revenge even if it is to hand. That is not enough for those men; they wish, in addition, to be received into our bosom just as if they had always shown themselves supremely trustworthy. Why is this? As people who have been cheated, treacherously betrayed, or cruelly outraged, are we not to venture to be on our guard in the future? But those men are penitent. Doubtless, since they are nothing but crocodiles, they wish confidence in their honesty to be gained with one small tear. Therefore, that inflexibility of ours is inhuman, because we do not spontaneously show ourselves indulgent[9] to them.

But I refrain from speaking about our private injuries. God will be gravely displeased. The offense is a recognized one and a trespass of the worst kind. Yes, and some people will heap crimes on crimes. Having been convicted, they admit half of the blame. After they have pled guilty, unless everything remains unchanged for them, as if they had never sinned, they bewail that they are being driven to despair by our severity. But when it is so sacred a matter, I maintain that penitence cannot be evaluated from lukewarm signs. Finally, how do they boast of penitence to me when they are not so humbled by recognition of their sin that they do not hesitate to present a brazen face in the pulpit [*in suggestum*] three days later? It has been the practice for monks to conceal, for the honor of their order, all the shameful deeds done among their cronies. Many might wish that this custom should be introduced into the Church of Christ, but I assert that the best way of taking care of the honor of the Christian name is to cleanse the temple of God of filth again.

Alleged License in the Reformed Church

But I have already wasted more than enough words in referring to calumnies by which scoundrels who have left us indirectly inflict wounds on the gospel through our side. I again

9. Reading *indulgentes* for *ingulandos,* which is meaningless. [tr.]

revert to calumnies of a general kind, by which manifest and avowed enemies openly attack our doctrine. In the first place, this is a common calumny with them, that under the pretext of Christian freedom we surrender to our own and other people's passion, and the only aim of our teaching is that men, set free from laws and discipline, may run riot without restriction and moderation. Our books will give ample conviction about what our teaching contains. But evidently it is as open to our enemies to lie among those who are prevented from reading our writings as it is superfluous for us to make excuses for ourselves before our readers.

225 But first of all I should like to know what is that yoke of discipline which is so grievous that it has forced us to fly to this refuge. For the severity of the papacy was never so great but that under it people were allowed all the year round to fornicate, to dance, to abandon themselves extravagantly to every luxury, to indulge in revelings, to play with dice, and to conduct themselves in every shameless way possible, provided that after a year's indulgence those who lived so badly went to a priest and unburdened themselves in his ear, as of the vomit of drunkenness. In such dissolute license, what then was the use of seeking this remedy of ultimate despair? Certainly, if there had ever been any desirous of new conditions, yet they did not begin to agitate to have their wish realized before, when there was then no hope in any other way. Indeed, no desire for wantonness could have titillated us were its impunity not permitted under the papacy.

But the praisers of the papacy are doubly absurd when they extol their own stern discipline and their Spartan practices. For who will trust a monk commending his own fasts with plump and rosy cheeks? Who will think of them as frugal when people everywhere know that they are immersed in restaurants? To conclude in a word, almost the whole of the papal clergy is a vast pit of crimes of every kind, which not only exhales its stench far and wide but also pollutes the remaining classes of society with a deadly contagion. But even if we concede that they have ordered everything purely[10] and chastely, they,

---

10. *Sancte.* 1550 has, wrongly, *fauste* ("favourably"). [B-N]

however, say that the purity of morals, which had been tight-
ened up by them, is being relaxed and loosened by us. To refute
this lie, the only witnesses I shall cite are those who annoy us
every day with their complaint that they have been deprived of
all their old liberty. I shall be saying nothing that is not well
known to all. You might say that all the licentious, extravagant,
and shameless men among us, who desire to allow what has
given them pleasure, are soldiers hired by the Pope in the fight
against the gospel. And they make no secret of the reason: that
this old and gloomy — as they call it — strictness, which
previously had lain obsolete in obscure writings, is something
quite intolerable to them. At least their attacks would have to
be abated, so that those good champions of self-restraint may
persuade them that we give to the flesh as much license
as it demands! But since those to whom the discipline of
the papacy would be pleasant and acceptable kick so much
against our severity, it will have been an easy matter for anyone
to conclude from this that our doctrine is very different from
that unrestrained indulgence of which they accuse it. Yes, and
what is more, many of the papists burden our doctrine with the
odium of stripping the world of nearly all its joy and merriment.

Three Particular Complaints

There are three things in particular that they cast up to us,
accusing us of having been longing for the liberty to do what we
like: (1) we have abolished auricular confession; (2) we have
condemned the prohibition of foods; and (3) we make the
practice of marriage open to all.

(1) Auricular Confession

They shout that the disgrace of sinning is abolished from the
world if the necessity of confession is not there holding it in
check. But it is a strange thing that both in the ancient Church
and throughout very many generations after the coming of
Christ, the Spirit of God made no use of this bridle. Shall we
therefore say that the whole of that time was free from guilt, so
that holiness, chastity, and all the virtues were particularly

226

flourishing? While the discipline was extremely stern and severe in those days, there was, however, no sign of this halter without which those worthy defenders of sobriety think there will be no salvation. But their boast that the passions of men are held in check by this remedy is false in the extreme. For who does not see that just as drunkards relieve themselves by vomiting, so that empty and fresh, as it were, they may go back quickly to new gluttony, so the papists spew their secret mutterings into the ear of a priest, so that, lightened of their former burden, they may the more boldly pile sins on sins. They do indeed say beforehand that they are confessing to God. But I maintain that they all have the same intention — baring their secrets privately to a priest so that they may be concealed from God and men. We thus observe that, with the clandestine murmuring behind them, they indulge themselves all the more carelessly. Besides, while we may grant that some are kept back by a servile fear, so that they abstain from sinning in order not to have the necessity of making their confession afterwards, they, however, maliciously infer that we are procuring the liberty of the flesh by doing this very thing. We condemn the law of Innocent,[11] which binds consciences with a necessity from which God absolves and delivers them. Let them expostulate with God, who so positively forbids anyone to fall into snares of that kind, so that he may not let souls — redeemed by the blood of Christ — be entangled. We maintain that impious audacity was the cause of the remission of sins being tied to a fiction of men. If we can defend his right and honor for Christ only by submitting to that reproach with which they brand us, then that is indeed an especially honorable thing for us. Certainly it is clear that those who conceive a scandal for themselves out of this are perverse and peevish.

(2) Foods

The excuse about the abolition of the distinction between foods is obvious and facile. They say that the flesh is given free

---

11. Pope Innocent III (1160-1216). See *Inst.*, III, iv, 7. "Decretals of Gregory IX" (1148-1241), lib. V, tit. 38 (*De poenitentiis et remissionibus*), ch. 12; for references, see *B-N*.

rein, so that it may indulge itself extravagantly, because we permit the eating of meats on Friday just the same as on Monday. As if the eating of meat is the only luxury there is! Moreover, who does not know that fish have always afforded greater pleasure, and that today kitchens are never smoking better or tables being laid more carefully or loaded with a greater variety or abundance than on fish days? Let there be no more of that nonsense that we attract simple souls with luxuries. For none of our number raises any question about more luxurious foods. But whereas the papists allow gluttony to be satisfied freely on a Friday with all sorts of delightful foods in abundance — with the sole exception of meat, pronouncing it unlawful to touch pork or beef — we leave ourselves the liberty granted to consciences by the Lord. Therefore, we boldly hold the principle that there is no more religious value in cheap intestines than in expensive, savory fish. Certainly we commend, as we should, a frugal and sober way of living, and nobody will find that our writings or discourses favor even so little of luxury. On the contrary, almost every single page of our writings will testify that we are a good deal more in advance of the papists in urging sobriety. And having done away with the superstition about days, we teach that we are at liberty to make careful and thrifty use of those things which, by the kindness of God, we have at hand. Is our delight in that liberty so great that it incites us to change the world? Certainly for my own part, if I were disposed to indulge my palate, I should choose other foods than meats for half the year. My friends know that I am extremely partial to fish and certain other things, from which I voluntarily abstain so as not to buy such pleasure at the expense of my health.

227

I confess that I feel ashamed to be refuting such trifling calumnies. But my readers will forgive me if, in my desire to meet stumbling blocks, I may be talking in frivolous vein. However, there is no need to waste any more time over these trifles. For this part of the doctrine which we teach consists of two parts. We strongly contend that it is wrong for consciences that ought to be ruled by the Word of God alone to be ensnared by human laws. Even if nothing were more beneficial than the habit of confession, we say that it is still impious presumption for men to impose a law which binds souls with religious scruples. For of right God arrogates it to himself alone that he is "our lawgiver and judge" (Jas. 4:12). At the same time we say that severe injury is done to Christ when the freedom acquired by his blood is thus reduced to nothing, for by his benefaction our condition is better than that of the people of old in this respect also — that we have been set free from the observance of days and foods. Thus we say along with Paul that the spiritual "kingdom of God is not in food and drink" (Rom. 14:17). Therefore, men are being deceived by perverse superstition when they think that part of holiness lies in abstaining from meats. Finally, we agree entirely with Paul, who clearly pronounces it a diabolical dogma to prohibit foods as if they were polluted, when God has consecrated them to the use of men, so that they may eat them freely "with thanksgiving" (I Tim. 4:1-5). No scandal is to be regarded so highly that one is at liberty to keep quietly hidden things that it is so vital to know.

This charge has not yet been completely disposed of, however, because our adversaries assert that we have nothing to do with the fasts which the Lord strongly and consistently commends. In the first place, since our books and discourses are strong enough in their protest against this reproach, little labor need be expended on its refutation here. Of course, they will object that we have abrogated the decrees already fixed long ago in regard to fasts. I admit that, and also indeed that even serious and important reasons have forced them to act most improperly, as they do when they turn into an offense the thing that we have undertaken piously and rightly.

It had been accepted as an ancient and common opinion that the Lenten fast originated from the institution of Christ.[12] It appears to be a trivial error, but an error nevertheless, and one not to be entertained. There is no difficulty at all in showing how foolish and absurd the thinking about that has been, and how rashly it has been believed. For if Christ intended to summon us to an annual fast by his own example, why did he carry it out only once in his whole life, and not every year? Why did he not institute the rite immediately among his disciples? Why — directly after his resurrection — did the apostles not

228

12. B-N gives references in Augustine and Jerome. [tr.]

keep the rule, as they would if it were prescribed by the Master? And why should the fast of Christ be imitated by us any more than Moses' fast was by the people of old? But which one of the prophets or the faithful drew an example from what was done by Moses?

Now take this other consideration into account, that it is an error such as can be disguised only at great cost to our faith. Nobody is in doubt that the doctrine of the gospel has been established as sacred[13] by that miracle, so that its authority would be the more assured. Accordingly, the gospel story recounts that Christ did not suffer hunger throughout the whole of the forty days. When the papists emulate what Christ accomplished in his divinity [*divinitus*] so that he might lift up reverence for his teaching above the human level, and they do so just as if it were subject to their own strength, are they not both obscuring the marvelous power of Christ as far as they are concerned, and blotting out that sacred sign by which the truth of the gospel had been confirmed?

As far as other fasts are concerned, we have no difficulty showing that when men thought that they were doing something pleasing to God they have in fact been demonstrating a crass veneration for idols. Scripture condemns as a perverse superstition the appointing of days to be honored by fasting. Establishing divine worship in that and imagining it a meritorious work is not only foolish and empty trust but pure impiety. If we follow Paul's lead, it will allow us to pronounce in general that "external exercises of that sort are of little value" (I Tim. 4:8),[14] for the substance of piety does not lie in them. Of course, this cannot be said without justly condemning that absolute rigor in enforcing fasting which holds sway among the papists, while they permit the neglect of necessary duties. Moreover, we can invoke words of the Master himself: "Hypocrites, for the sake of your traditions you make void the commandments of God" (Matt. 15:6f.).[15] Now when more serious causes are impelling us to speak, suddenly, however, they make us advocates of gluttony and intemperance of every kind.

---

13. *Sanctam fuisse,* amending *sancitam* in B-N.
14. *RV,* "bodily exercise." [tr.]
15. *B-N* has Matt. 15:3. [tr.]

229 Although those people with whom I am now in dispute are shamelessly impudent, they ought to be countered with so just and serious a defense. For I ask you, what law does the Pope ordain for his fast days? That a man is not to taste food before midday; that he abstain from meat; and finally, that being content with luncheon alone he do without supper that day. Furthermore, this is the usual procedure: on the preceding day they go to sleep well filled, so that the fasting of a couple of hours might be more tolerable; on the fast day itself, because luncheon is the only meal allowed them, they gorge themselves freely; on the day following it, they avenge themselves with unrestrained and excessive drinking of wine. After they have played with God as fearlessly as if he were any child, they also add to their pile of wickedness this claim that we have completely abandoned a frugal way of living. I genuinely maintain that while they are dissolute in the whole of life, nowhere, however, do they run more stupidly into bestial intemperance than in their fasts.

(3) Marriage

Something still remains to be said about marriage. Our adversaries suppose that we have stirred up something like a Trojan War on account of women. I must pass over other men at present so that they may concede that I at least am free from that reproach. Therefore, I have greater freedom to rebut their offensive prattle. While I was always free to marry a wife when I was under the papal tyranny, from the time that the Lord snatched me out of it I voluntarily led a celibate life for several years. It is now eighteen months since the death of my wife,[16] a woman of matchless type, and ever since I have again been practicing celibacy, and not unwillingly. These things will perhaps seem to contribute little to the subject; but I was disposed to put them down by way of a brief preface, partly in order that the slanderous falsehood of our enemies might be refuted by them and partly that it might be shown to all that I am at least pleading a private case.

16. Calvin was married in 1540; his wife died in 1549. [tr.]

But what do those worthy defenders of chastity allege? They assert that Luther and others, urged on by the itching of the flesh, not only created the freedom of marriage for themselves but also dragged a multitude of priests, monks, and nuns into the same allurements. I deliberately pass over the truth which could be revealed about the continence of individuals whom they accuse spitefully and falsely. For is there anything more ridiculous than fleeing from the papacy because they cannot endure to live chastely? In other words, there was no freedom for priests, monks, and nuns to satisfy their lust unless they sought a fresh asylum for themselves far from the highest difficulties. As if indeed all the cells and all the seats and bookcases of monks and nuns do not stink with fornication of all sorts. I am not touching upon unnatural lusts here. But what is the point of concealing something notorious, so to banish modesty and shame from certainly the majority of those caves, in order that the good fathers might have at least some freedom to indulge in fornication there? What am I to say about the priests who feel no shame for their lusts, to such an extent that it is now a glorious thing for them to set up the signs [*trophaea*] of them everywhere? Certainly, to put it at the lowest, it is not necessary to go outside the papacy for those who like women.

Yet I do not absolutely deny that many monks fly out of their cages so that they may openly obtain among us the sexual love 230 which they snatch there in secret. But I shall venture to cite those very men as witnesses of how far removed marriage is from the sensual life which they used to lead in brothels. Accordingly, because some detect at once how much more restricting is the chaste cohabitation of a man with a wife than the promiscuous lasciviousness of the papal celibacy, they beat a hasty retreat back to their former nests. Others, more desperate, migrate to Rome — or wherever fate draws them. And indeed this is one of the angelic virtues of the cloistered! That apart, when I concede that many perversely abuse our teaching, it must be obvious how the cause of the scandal is still justified.

God established mankind according to this law: that the man maintain the position of head over the woman, and the woman, on the other hand, be a helper to the man; and so at the same time he bound both sexes together in a mutual bond. Before men had been corrupted, marriage was bestowed on them — and allowed them — as a unique blessing. We maintain that it is intolerable that this blessing of God be snatched away from mortal man. Now on account of the incontinence of the flesh, there has been even greater necessity for this, the primary institution of God. For not for nothing does the Spirit, speaking through Paul, prescribe this remedy for avoiding fornication: that "every man have his own wife, and every single woman also have her own husband" (I Cor. 7:2). Not for nothing do Christ and the same Paul warn that all are not fitted for, and capable of the celibate life (Matt. 19:11f.; I Cor 7:7-9). And one would wish that less was known of the disease of incontinency in this degenerate nature.

In order to provide help for this failing, not only did God institute marriage, in which a man may live lawfully with a woman, but he clearly invites all who burn on account of the flesh to the legitimate use of it (I Cor. 7:9). Apostles, martyrs, and others, the most eminent among the saints, have used this benefit. The admiration of celibacy that suddenly appeared has had the result that the honor and dignity of marriage have become worthless.[17] However, there was voluntary abstention from marriage for a time until superstition opened the door to tyranny. Accordingly, priests were debarred from married life. In the end the ban gradually spread to deacons. Monks and nuns, caught in the grip of an oath, renounced for themselves the right granted by God. Hence the world began to think that celibates are the only people sacred to God. Fierce madness has proceeded so far that they treat married life with serious dishonor, as if it were something profane. Even if a change of that sort at first appeared to work out favorably, we still maintain that it has its source in a presumption that is of the devil. In fact, the holier the virtue of chastity is, the more vicious and the more detestable is that forced celibacy which is plainly crammed full of every kind of foul filth. Since all who are averse to marriage appear to be like angels, the papists extol virginity with marvelous encomiums.

17.   *Inst.*, IV, xii, 27.

Indeed, it is as if — outside the married state — they have demonstrated all that is chaste and virginal. But in this situation they appear to have beds without wives of their own, only so that they themselves may lie and violate other men's wives. For who does not know their common saying: "Since a monk or priest is debarred from the common right of marrying a wife, it is right and proper for him to provide for himself in another way"? And so that they may not fail in their duties, almost all strenuously devote themselves to this kind of sexual indulgence. No snare is better suited to their pandering ways than confession, for they use it not only to make women their accomplices in any adulterous act, and put them under obligation to themselves, but to do a service [assignant] to one another. Therefore, it has come to this, that those who are satisfied by domestic harlots are thought to be chaste and self-disciplined among others. I omit secret obscenities and abominable acts of lewdness. And indeed I would not even mention these things, although they are generally known, except that it is necessary that my readers be reminded in passing how uprightly the adversaries of our doctrine behave at the same time that they accuse it of dissolute license, seeing that it allows lawful marriage for the correcting of such horrible evils.

Even if those who do not cease to honor the forced celibacy of the papal clergy with feigned praises were silenced, yet it is evident that the majority of them constitute the most loathsome abyss of every kind of filth; but I maintain that those who seem to be continent are just as foul a pit. Of course, God punishes that devilish presumption not only with such hidden flames of passions but also with such open deeds of shame, because, disdaining the blessing of marriage, they rear up towers of Babel like the giants, by which they may overcome nature and God. And this had to happen so that men might learn at least that true chastity is the very thing that the rule of God prescribes for us. But because we hold our animal passions in check by the bridle of marriage, while there is no restriction on these in the papacy, we are said to declare liberty for the flesh and to remove all modesty of behavior. And why should that cause surprise, since both Christ and Paul were accused of something similar, as if they had taken pains to remove the yoke of the Law so that men's own will might be the law for them? For they would not have been so careful about clearing their teaching of calumnies if they had not been forced to do so by the wickedness and poisonous wantonness of their enemies. Moreover, I am confident that all those who are curable have been won over by this brief defense, so that they may not invent a scandal for themselves out of such a trivial and silly matter.

Alleged Break With Antiquity

There is also some justification for the scandal that our teaching is in conflict with antiquity and the agreement of all the centuries. [18] The papists accordingly take very great pride in that, especially when they blow their trumpets and intone those great names of the Fathers and the Church. Since it is well enough known how newness in religion is odious and suspect, they frighten away the inexperienced from our doctrine with a pretext of this sort. And I certainly admit that if anything new is introduced it is given a poor hearing.

But there is no better or more certain way to get rid of this calumny than our wish that nothing be accepted except what is approved by clear and firm scriptural testimonies. And even in this it appears that the papists are more stupid than oxen and asses, which do at least know their own stalls; for since they have fashioned a new God for themselves, they have so forgotten the one true and eternal God that they have no taste for the antiquity of the heavenly oracles. Yet they object that Scripture is falsely pled as an excuse by us in our attempt to overthrow the complete unanimity of the early Church. Indeed that is a well-worn calumny among them, but one so offensive that it annoys me to waste much time in refuting it. Indeed a long book would be needed for that purpose. And our books abundantly testify — if the opinions of the men of old are being sought — that our cause is helped rather than damaged by them. Al-

18. *Ibid.*, IV, xii, 26, 28. (The reference here is confined to celibacy and marriage. — tr.)

though it is well enough known that the teaching of the men of old is no more in accord with the corruptions of the papacy than a sheep is like a wolf, yet they sometimes appropriate certain sayings and even little words of theirs, perversely as well as wrongly, and by doing so they may deceive the ignorant and those who are not practiced in the reading of those men.

Whenever we present them with the testimonies of the Fathers, even if they may see that they are overwhelmed in weight and number, yet as they appear to themselves to be placed completely out of range of any weapon, they carelessly make light of it and laugh. For the Apostolic Seat, in its greatness, easily swallows all the Teachers that ever were. And nothing is easier for them than this exception, that they care nothing for any opinions of the Fathers when a different pronouncement has been made from the Holy Roman throne. Therefore, the whole company of the Fathers will indeed be valued at less than a straw among them, unless they choose otherwise. On the other hand, anything that through scant attention escapes the memory of any of them will immediately bind our consciences so much [*tanta religione*] that it would be sinful to differ even in the slightest. I again repeat that that confused and prodigious chaos of the papacy is unlike the ancient regime of the Church every bit as much as fire differs from water. Even if we appear to be too ardent and noisy in condemning it, the vehemence of the Fathers would be far greater if they were alive today.

Take into account also that those worthy sons who playfully toss the name of the Fathers about as though playing with a ball seem to have taken pains to pick out all the most stupid errors, and if we do not agree with them they shout out that we are hostile to the whole of antiquity. For example, Melchizedek brought out bread and wine to Abraham when he was returning from battle [Gen. 14:18]. The ancients think that this was a sacrifice, which they transferred to the Holy Supper of Christ. That is almost childish hallucination. Yet, out of such very clear lucubrations of theirs nothing pleases the papists as much. So that I may not be too long now in this section, those who are versed in the writings of the Fathers and form a moderate judgment understand well enough that we are supported by

233   their authority for fighting against the papists. Certainly to get a public decision they will, however, attack us more closely.

What, then, gives rise to such a massive scandal? And even if we may concede that the pure truth of God cannot be defended and restored by us without that unanimity of many centuries — which they praise — raising itself in opposition (I acknowledge how, for a thousand years, everything has fallen in ruins, so that monstrous errors and superstitions have repeatedly emerged), yet what do they find in such disagreement that merits such a great stumbling block? If a comparison is to be made, certainly those first men under whom the Church flourished either deserve to be regarded as the only legitimate Fathers or rightly claim for themselves at least the principal position of honor among the Fathers. But the worthy papists (such is their ingenuousness) commemorate only that more corrupt age, which had already deviated far from the purity of ancient times. And all their complaints finally come back to this, that the usage accepted for eight hundred or a thousand years is today being overthrown by us. Nevertheless, if the old proverb, which has been familiar even among us, is to be believed, "bad custom is nothing else but long-standing error."[19] Moreover, the longer the evil lasts the more deadly we know it to be. This saying of Cyprian was once acceptable: "We must not look at what others did and said before us, but we must follow what Christ, who is the first of all, has commanded."[20] Also, nobody used to deny Augustine's beautiful and shrewd dictum: "Christ does not give Himself the name Custom but Truth."[21]

Nobody now dares to disturb even slightly that chamber of corrupt practice which has lain quiet through the long succession of years. On the contrary, inflexible rigor in preserving the greatest absurdities has prevailed even to the point that not only do they reject the censure of them, as though it were untimely, but they take cruel revenge with fire and sword. The ancient heathen man says, "As the habit of speaking properly is to be sought from the learned, so also that of living is to be

19.   Cyprian, *Ep.*, LXXIV, 9.
20.   *Ibid.*, LXIII, 14.
21.   Augustine, *De Baptismo contra Donatistas*, III, 6.

sought from the good and upright."[22] Will a vicious and corrupt human institution sweep us away like some violent tempest, without discretion or distinction, from Christ who is our director? I must conclude this topic briefly. Without any argument it ought to be an axiom among the devout that the doctrine of Christ is not to be subjected to the rule of years. If that has force among us, then that fictitious scandal will not keep anyone back from at least the endeavor to make inquiries. But when it is established that what we make known we have from Christ, who will be so absurd as to go of his own accord to men, away from the eternal wisdom of God and the voice of the heavenly Teacher?

The Title "The Church"

It is an offense to a great many people that they see almost the whole world opposed to us. And indeed the patrons of a bad cause do not neglect their own advantage, using a stratagem like this so as not to upset the ignorant and weak, that it is extremely absurd that almost the whole Christian world is disregarded, so that the faith is to be possessed by a few men. But, in particular, to destroy us they defend themselves with the sacred title of "the Church" as if with a mallet. But I wish to know how those who are alienated from the gospel by the smallness of our numbers are to preserve their faith against the Turks.

234

As far as we are concerned, if one man, Noah, condemned all the men of his generation by his faith, there is no reason why a great crowd of unbelievers should move us from our position. At the same time, I say that it is not only hardly a probable, but indeed an unjust and disgraceful, cause of a scandal when regard for men outweighs the Word of God. What then? Will the truth of God not stand unless we have been pleased to put our confidence in men? On the contrary, as Paul says, "Let man remain the liar that he is. Let those to whom God deigns to reveal himself, know that he is true" (Rom. 3:4). And we have already shown elsewhere why the majority of men are so reluctant about yielding themselves in obedience to God. Therefore,

22.   Quintilian, *Inst. orat.*, I, vi, 45. For full references, see *B-N*.

when the world shows such obstinacy it is by no means appropriate that our faith be directed according to the example of the multitude. Moreover, the sign is given by Christ, "where the eagles gather together there the body is" (Matt. 24:28). I do not deny indeed that if all the eagles ever gathered together in one place, the conversion of the whole world is to be looked for at once. But since Christ is not meaning there all eagles in general, but those which follow the life-giving odor of his death, who does not see that the expression must be restricted to a few men? If anyone perhaps objects that we are not excused by the example of Noah, if we separate ourselves from that crowd which keeps the name of "the Church," Isaiah, when he gave orders to abandon the conspiracy of men and follow God alone, was referring not to strangers but to those who were at that time glorying exceedingly in the name of the people of God (Isa. 8:12). And when Peter compares the Church to the ark, because in a perishing world a small company of men is saved as if through a flood, he is giving warning enough that we must not be dependent on the multitude (I Pet. 3:20ff.). Why then does it please wretched men to grasp at the chance of staggering and tottering in the changeable breezes of the world when God makes us firm on the eternal foundation of his Word? Why do they prefer to be tossed about in the midst of the storms of opinions rather than lie quietly in the safe harbor of certain truth, where God invites us?

Yet the highest reverence is due to the Church. Of course I agree; and I am glad to add also that the idea of the Church is so connected with the genuine doctrine of the law and gospel that it is deservedly called the faithful guardian and interpreter of it. But this is the difference between us and the papists. They think that the Church is "the pillar of the truth" (I Tim. 3:15), just as if it controls the Word of God. On the other hand, we assert that the truth is possessed by the Church and handed down to others because it subjects itself reverently to the Word of God. Accordingly, the Word of God has no more authority among them than the Church allows it, as if by favor, and they alter the interpretation of the whole of Scripture according to the judgment of the Church, just as the old proverb tells that the Lesbians were once accustomed to shaping stone according to

235

their leaden rule.[23] Therefore, there is no passage of Scripture so clear that, bent or, to speak more correctly, distorted according to this Lesbian rule, does not assume another form.

Yet it is not here that we are engaged in the most important struggle. But after the papists have set up the Church on the throne of Christ, so that it establishes religion by its own authority, and makes judgments on Scripture without challenge, they then seize that right, whatever it is, for themselves. Indeed, because it is as easy as it is dangerous to be deceived in this matter, we wish that it be determined which is the true Church. It is certainly no new thing for those who take charge in the office of pastor sometimes to be "cruel wolves" (Acts 20:29), and for those who have customary power in their hands to be ungodly and treacherous betrayers of God and the Church. Why then do lifeless specters frighten us away from investigating, as is proper, whether what is called "the Church" is truly the Church? Paul says that the Church is "the pillar of the truth" (I Tim. 3:15), but he also predicts the rebellion of the already converted world and the open reign of Antichrist in the temple of God (II Thess. 2:4).[24] It is known well enough that he had to undergo the same struggles by which we are exercised today, when the Jews, taking pride in the name of "the Church," were loud in their complaints that he was both an apostate and the cause of schisms and disturbances.

They boast that they are descended in continuous succession all the way from the apostles themselves, doubtless just as Caligula and Nero succeeded Valerius Publicola and Lucius Brutus! For they connect themselves to the apostles in this way, as if there had not intervened the immense chaos of disagreement which broke off whatever links there ever were. Because the dregs of the Roman clergy are against us, they intend us to feel as annoyed by that precedent as if the angels condemned us out of heaven. Of course, the scribes once repudiated Christ

23. Aristotle, *Nicomachean Ethics*, V, x, 7. "What is itself indefinite can only be measured by an indefinite standard, like the leaden rule used by Lesbian builders; just as that rule is not rigid but can be bent to the shape of the stone, so a special ordinance is made to fit the circumstances of the case" (Eng. trans. by H. Rackham, Loeb Classical Library, London, 1947). [tr.]
24. See *Inst.*, IV, vii, 25; IV, ix, 4.

with the same contempt because none of the rulers and the Pharisees had believed in him. And indeed it is no wonder that those men rant on with empty sounds, since they are determined to fight stubbornly right to the bitter end on behalf of their own tyranny, and that they are destitute of genuine grounds. But I wish all those who regard it as a scandal that the name of "the Church" has been falsely appropriated to be asked to bear to open their ears and eyes at last, so that the deceptive representation of the body may not tear them away from the head, so that the prostitute, embellished with the adornments of a bride, may not rob them of Christ, the bridegroom. For I beseech you, what marks do they have from which they may recognize the Church of Christ in the entire crowd of the Roman Antichrist? Unless perhaps when they see the Pope arrayed in white and a cross reaching to his feet,[25] cardinals clothed in purple, bishops conspicuous with mitre and crosier, and the remainder — the lesser crowd — distinct in their own insignia also, they are content with these tokens and have no great desire for any other church than the one appearing in theatrical displays.

For what else is left to be said to those worthless fellows who, having been refuted so often and so severely and fully by us, yet still continue to arrogate the title of "the Church" to themselves. I said at the beginning[26] that almost the only people who are deceived in this connection are those who are unwilling to give their assent to Christ and make far-fetched obstacles for themselves. There was indeed a time when this difficulty hindered many simple and pious souls, but I maintain that today not a few oppose sound doctrine with a stumbling block from the name of "the Church" so as to insult Christ maliciously and proudly.[27] The same kind of impudence causes them to press for miracles, so that, having been reduced to astonishment by them, they may be forced at last to yield to God speaking through us. In fact, I say that while our doctrine offers clear-shining evidence for itself, it has been established

25. This seems the best rendering of the ambiguous *et proiectam ad eius pedes crucem*. The reference is to a vestment. See G. Barraclough, *The Medieval Papacy* (London, 1968), pp. 45, 64, illus. [tr.]

26. Presumably pp. 13-14 and 89 above.

27. To clarify the litotes here, *non* is transferred from *malitiose* (final clause) to *paucos*. [tr.]

by all the miracles which have appeared since the foundation of the world; and since those men who have forgotten the ancient miracles to gape at new ones are so dumbfounded at the open power of God, and blind in the clear light of day, I maintain that they are monstrosities, just as if we were to see a man turned into an animal.

Accusation of Robbery

Since a few have been enriched by sacred wealth, while others have somehow checked their greed for the time being, the enemies of the gospel assert that we have been prompted to change things more by a passion for plunder than by a pious zeal for God. Many who are eager for a pretext to reject the gospel agree with those slanderers. Certainly I make no excuses if any have plundered the goods of the Church to fill their own purses. And our books are eloquent witnesses of how much we stand in horror of such sacrileges. Yet, as it is not my intention to undertake the defense of crimes on our side, if there are any, so the calumny is not to be tolerated when malevolent men make the accusation that whatever has been taken away from those infamous spendthrifts, namely the priests of Baal and the monks, was equivalent to booty. Certainly in those places where the ungodliness of the papacy has been brought to an end, there at least part of those revenues, which prostitutes and pimps used to devour along with the priests, is disbursed on the poor; much more is being devoted to schools than used to be done; true pastors who provide the people with the doctrine of salvation are being maintained; and a good deal of expense is also incurred in maintaining the Church's state. Although this defense may not absolve us in the sight of God (and indeed I freely confess as much), it is being shown that a scandal is however spitefully constructed from this against the doctrine of the gospel. But they declare that it is being made public why we have been driven voluntarily to undertake this defense: it is 237 because almost all are busy looking after their own private affairs and are sluggish in enforcing discipline, in correcting faults, in advancing and upholding the Kingdom of Christ. Why, then, do they not fire us with their own ardor instead of

113

they themselves freezing at our coldness? Let Haggai's complaints about neglect of the temple be read (Hag. 1). There one may see the sloth of our times set out as in a picture. Because at that time everyone was intent on his own home and was not caring about the temple of God, did that mean that God's work — the restoration of the temple — was not sacrosanct? Should anyone have grown weary because he was seeing others not only giving up in a necessary duty but also wickedly defrauding God of first fruits and tithes? But of course this is what I have already said in the introduction,[28] that many have got entangled in the profane friendships of the world and seize upon any stumbling block at all against Christ rather than offend people who are ungodly and inimical to sound doctrine. This perverse ambition supplies those men with a genius for fabricating scandals, and with eloquence for tearing the gospel to pieces with dog's abuse.

In addition, not content with biting at our present faults, they pry into the future to gnaw at it with the same malignity. For they make out that in their opinion they foresee that the Church is close to ruin, which is threatening from internal disagreements. Prudent men are amazed that we are not more affected by this; and indeed, in order to drag us into odium, they conclude that it does not matter to us if the world is embroiled in flames. Thus I remember the Bishop of Aquila once arguing with me in a private conversation how a dreadful calamity would have to be feared if we did not bring dissensions to an end soon. But his whole speech amounted to this: if we were so persistent in our purpose, it was bound to happen that the matter would finally come to arms. Moreover, the only outcome of the war would be that, good learning having been destroyed and barbarous disorder introduced, humanity itself would almost be removed from the world. As the blame for these misfortunes would stick to us, so the odium must be endured. "Yes indeed," he said, "this very religion for which you fight so eagerly is bound to perish at the same time as learning."

28. Pp. 13-14 above.

114

What I then said in reply to one man, let all accept as if I spoke to them: we are certainly neither so dull that all Satan's contrivances do not enter our mind, nor so barbarous and inhuman that we do not care in the slightest. Not only do we desire a plan for peace and tranquillity but we do take counsel for them, as far as it depends on us. We are no less devoted to order and polity than anyone else. There is no need to put into words how much concern for learning disturbs us. But since Christ has ordered that the gospel be preached with no exception placed in its way, this command must be obeyed, no matter what the result may be. However, men arrogate too much to themselves if they expect better success from their own   238 plans than from the procedure prescribed for them by God. What then? Do they suppose that God is blind and inconsiderate to expose his Church rashly to dangers? On the contrary, since he is the supremely good governor of all things, it is our duty to overcome difficulties, however perplexing, with this one saying to Abraham: "The Lord will provide" (Gen. 22:8). Of course, we shall be anxious about human society; but will God, its Creator, be untouched by concern for it? Wretchedly abandoned by the sole guardian and protector of its salvation, will the Church fall back on our providence? Surely we deserve to be excused if, by obediently carrying out the task that is laid on us, we leave his part to God. And when David says that it is his own particular work to calm the turbulent waves of the sea, "to make wars to cease, and to break chariots and spears" (Ps. 46), this confidence ought rightly to encourage us to defend that doctrine which alone procures for us his grace and blessing. Yet, whatever result may at length follow our efforts, there never will be reason to regret that we showed both pious and grateful obedience to God, and, what will be able to relieve our sorrow even in the greatest catastrophes, that we faithfully served both the glory of Christ, which is preferable to all the kingdoms of the world, and the salvation of souls, which is more precious than the whole world.

CONCLUSION

AFTER GOING OVER by classes the scandals that we know by experience are doing most harm at present, I must now briefly warn the sons of God again, that, having been provided with the remedies I have shown, they retain Christ as a foundation rather than, by a rash and improper attack, make him "a stone of stumbling and a rock of offence" for themselves. It is inevitable that many scandals are inflicted upon the faithful time and again in this world, since not even Christ was immune from them. Indeed, one can scarcely expect them to take a single step without Satan putting some scandal in their way. So they must walk through innumerable stumbling blocks. But however numerous, varied, and thickly piled they may be, yet nobody will be a Christian unless he emerges victorious. Christ himself said that Peter was a scandal for him when Peter attempted to keep him back from submitting to death. But having been attacked, did Christ retreat from the stumbling block? No, rather — perceiving Satan in Peter — he ordered him to get behind him (Matt. 16:23). So that we may realize that we shall share the struggle with him, Christ states in general terms that "it is necessary for scandals to come" (Matt. 18:7).

But just as he promises that his own will never be free from scandals, so he does not excuse anything that causes a scandal. For when he orders "the right eye to be plucked out if it causes
239　anyone to stumble" (Matt. 5:29), he is warning that nothing is to be of such importance that regard for it ought to deflect us

from the goal in the slightest degree. If we were so careful about guarding against scandals that none of us spared even our own eyes, there would be no need at all for me to expend so much labor in removing scandals. I admit that the battle is arduous and beyond our own strength, but not for nothing does Christ say that he has spoken to his disciples so that they "should not be made to stumble" (John 16:1). For it is only because we do not hear Christ speaking that we are not equal to conquering and putting an end to scandals. What he says in another passage is certainly true, that those who stumble, "stumble in the night" (John 11:10).[1] But what is the purpose of the light of the gospel except that by showing the way it also simultaneously exposes scandals to our view? But someone will say, "Even if the barrier is seen, yet it does not cease to block the way." Indeed, I have already shown[2] that, unless our own softness hinders us, Christ alone suffices for overcoming any scandals whatever, since he lifts us up above the world by his heavenly power.

But if there must be such strong resistance to a scandal that confronts those who are reluctant and ready to run, there is less excuse for those who are actually inclined toward scandals through a certain perversity of mind. Paul warns that that is what happened to the Jews. Since they openly snatched at the slightest scandal, and because, "wishing to establish their own, they did not however submit to the righteousness of God" (Rom. 10:3), they "stumbled over" Christ (Rom. 9:32)[3] and indeed came to grief as if on a rock in fatal shipwreck. Certainly the perversity of those who gladly seize upon scandals presented to them, or even eagerly fetch them from far afield, is quite intolerable. What then? When Paul asserts that he is "forgetting the life that lies behind him to press on to the prize of the high calling," and encourages us by his example to make similar haste (Phil. 3:13-17), will anyone search for distant scandals to cause delay on the road, and do so with impunity?

Now, if God has so severely punished perverted zeal in the case of the Jews, what, do we imagine, will there be for those who

1. *Offendere eos qui offendunt.*
2. See p. 20; also p. 45.
3. Cf. *RSV* [tr.]

knowingly and willingly stumble, and what indeed for those who bury the otherwise plain road with stumbling blocks thick on every side? In particular, what forgiveness do those people leave for themselves who, to repel God, make shields for themselves out of the faults or crimes of men? For if even believers themselves are forbidden to look at each other, in case anything might check their speed, how would Christ pardon us if we cast our eyes far and wide, carefully searching for anything that might detain us? And one can indeed really and truly compare such people to pigs, for, on account of their natural love of filth, there is nothing that gives them greater pleasure than rolling themselves in mud and dung. The dire punishment of God awaits all the pigs who are far too eager for scandals, whether they hunt for them or rejoice that they are put before them, so that stumbling blocks, daily piled one on top of the other, plunge them into eternal destruction. For it is right that those who choose to be blind are so seriously blinded[4] that their disease is, in the end, incurable.

240

As for ourselves, in the meantime, since we hear Christ cursing all who cause a scandal for the weak (Luke 17:1f.), let us be anxious and careful that no stumbling block at all may occur through our fault. Otherwise, seeing that Christ must be "a stone of offence" (Rom. 9:32f.) to the reprobate and to an unbelieving world, only let us be beyond reproach in removing stumbling blocks intrepidly, as often as Satan brings them up, or else let us be protected by that title of Christ alone. At the same time, let us recall another of Christ's sayings. For when the disciples had objected that the Pharisees were offended, he directed that the latter be quietly disregarded because they were "blind, and leaders of the blind" (Matt. 15:12, 14). He also added a remarkable word: "Every plant which my Father has not planted will be rooted out" (Matt. 15:13). Thus our undoubted course of action is to be anxious for the salvation of all, as far as we can, but because it has not been granted to us to save those whom God has destined for destruction, "what is perishing, let it perish," as Zechariah has it (Zech. 11:9). For if Paul had been willing to remove the stumbling block of the

---

4. *Excaecari*, correcting 1550's wrong reading, *exsecrari*. [B-N]

cross, it would have been easy to compose some indirect reasons for this. But he stands in such horror of this intention that he considers it the height of absurdity if it is removed (I Cor. 1:17). Clearly, he regarded what he says in another passage as something fixed, that "although we are an odor from death to death to the reprobate, we nevertheless breathe a sweet aroma to God" (II Cor. 2:15-17).

LAUS DEO.